I Believe ...

THE APOSTLES' CREED
FOR THE THIRD MILLENNIUM

Foundations of the Faith

"Foundations of the Faith" is a series designed to explore and explain the basic doctrines of the Christian faith. Planned future volumes include studies of the Ten Commandments and the Lord's Prayer. It is our hope that lay people and ministers will find these resources useful not only in developing their own faith, but in their ministries of preaching, teaching and witnessing.

I Believe ...

THE APOSTLES' CREED
FOR THE THIRD MILLENNIUM

ROBERT P. MILLS

PLC Publications

I BELIEVE ...
THE APOSTLES' CREED
FOR THE THIRD MILLENNIUM

© 1998 PLC Publications

PO Box 2210
Lenoir, NC 28645

Cover and layout design by Tina Tallent

First printing
ISBN 0-9652602-2-4
Library of Congress Catalogue Number 98-92020

PRINTED IN THE UNITED STATES OF AMERICA

Contents

THE SPIRIT AND THE CHURCH

Introduction

As Christianity approaches its third millennium, Christians around the world continue to confess their faith by reciting a creed that can trace its origins to the first century A.D.

Why?

Why is the Apostles' Creed still used by God's people in their corporate worship and private devotion? What purposes are served by today's affirmations of this ancient statement of faith? Indeed, why should third-millennium Christians spend valuable time studying a creed that is almost 2,000 years old?

Root and fruit

One benefit of studying the Apostles' Creed is connecting ourselves to what all Christians everywhere have always believed. In so doing we remind ourselves that despite ever-changing social circumstances Christian faith is not ours to redefine. Being deeply rooted in "the faith that was once for all entrusted to the saints" (Jude 3) is essential to the life and ministry of God's people (Psalm 1:1-3).

Studying this historic creed also moves us forward in our faith. For as we develop a deeper understanding of its teachings, we thereby grow in our knowledge of Scripture and ultimately our knowledge of God. Such knowledge helps us keep in step with the Holy Spirit. It allows our lives to be good soil from which God can bring forth much fruit (Matt 13:23; Gal. 5:22-25). Knowing Scripture and knowing God also enable us to obey Peter's instruction to "be prepared to give an answer to everyone who asks you to give the reason for the hope that you have" (I Peter 3:15).

An invaluable resource

Originally taught to converts preparing for baptism (see Chapter 2), the Apostles' Creed remains an invaluable resource for individuals of any age, or at any stage of faith development, who want to learn more about what Christians everywhere have always believed. It provides a compact summary of many of the most important elements of Christian faith and life.

These studies begin with an introductory section on the nature of faith, the purpose of creeds, and the place of doubt. The remaining sections follow the order of the Creed and consider what the Creed has to teach about God the Father, God the Son, and God the Holy Spirit. Each chapter looks at a single article, or at times a single word, seeking to understand how the Creed is rooted in Scripture, how it has been understood throughout church history, and how it remains relevant.

The chapters conclude with questions for reflection and a suggested prayer for personal or corporate response. A list of Scripture passages for further study and additional resources are also included at the end of each chapter. The questions and Scripture readings make each chapter a suitable lesson for a Sunday School class, communicant's class, or other group study.

Preparing these studies afforded me a wonderful opportunity to reimmerse myself in the most basic beliefs of the Christian faith. I pray that those who read this book will also be refreshed as they contemplate the foundations of the faith.

Many of these chapters originated as sermons preached at the Big Creek Presbyterian Church in Rensselaer, Mo. More recently, they appeared as part of the "Foundations of the Faith" series in *The Presbyterian Layman*. I am grateful to the members of the Big Creek church and the staff, members and supporters of the Presbyterian Lay Committee who have encouraged the development and publication of these studies.

The Apostles' Creed

I believe in God the Father Almighty, Maker of heaven and earth.

And in Jesus Christ his only Son our Lord; who was conceived by the Holy Ghost, born of the Virgin Mary, suffered under Pontius Pilate, was crucified, dead, and buried; he descended into hell; the third day he rose again from the dead; he ascended into heaven, and sitteth on the right hand of God the Father Almighty; from thence he shall come to judge the quick and the dead.

I believe in the Holy Ghost; the holy catholic Church; the communion of saints; the forgiveness of sins; the resurrection of the body; and the life everlasting. Amen.

1

THE NATURE
OF FAITH

Suggested Scripture readings
Mark 9:14-29; Hebrews 11:1-10

The father of a demon-possessed boy brought his son to
Jesus' disciples, who tried but failed to drive the demon out.
Disillusioned and despairing the father cried out to Jesus, "If
you are able to do anything, have pity on us and help us."
Jesus replied, "All things are possible for the one who
believes." Immediately the father responded, "I believe ..."

Every Sunday countless Christians around the world echo
this father's faith as they recite an ancient creed that begins
with the words "I believe." But what, exactly, does it mean
for a contemporary Christian to affirm "I believe ..."? Or,
to state the question in theological terms, What is the nature
of faith?

Faith

In the New Testament the Greek *pisteuo*, from a root
meaning "trusting, worthy of trust," underlies the English
words "believe," "belief" and "faith." Various New Testament authors use this word to convey not only belief but also
obedience, trust, faithfulness, and hope. In writing about the
difficulties of translating this term Edward Dowey observes:

It is unfortunate that we cannot say in English 'I faith in God,' as is done in New Testament Greek or in German. The trouble with 'believe' is that it is too mental or theoretical to represent adequately the trust that is part of faith. John Baillie distinguished between believing from the top of the mind and believing from the bottom of the heart, which is faith. Faith, in the New Testament sense, includes knowing, but goes beyond what can be merely known.

Diogenes Allen draws a similar distinction:

Faith is not a particular feeling or emotion, so that one might conduct a search to determine whether one has had such a feeling or experience. One may, for example, have been 'born again' and experienced an immense thrill. I personally have known such a thrill, but to experience such a thrill is not essential to having faith because some people have never had such an experience and yet they have faith. In Christianity, faith involves the recognition and acceptance of God's saving work in Jesus Christ. To recognize the good that God intends for us to receive is to have experienced God's grace; faith is our consent to receive that good.

'Triple-A Faith'

John Brokhoff uses an alliterative approach to the nature of faith as affirmed in the Apostles' Creed. He refers to "Triple-A Faith," with the first 'A' being:

Assent. This is an intellectual admission, that a certain person or thing exists. It is the acceptance of a fact or reality. This is the easiest part of faith. It is an admission which does not require any responsibility about what you believe.

Faith as assent gives content to our faith. What then shall we believe? We believe in giving assent to the truths that God is our creating Father, that Jesus is the Christ, and that the Holy Spirit is God our Comforter. When we say 'I believe,' we are agreeing to the truths contained in the Apostles' Creed. This is what we Christians believe.

"To recognize the good that God intends for us to receive is to have experienced God's grace; faith is our consent to receive that good."
— *Diogenes Allen*

Attitude is Brokhoff's second 'A.'

Many people stop in their faith with assent, but this is not enough to believe. Faith goes beyond intellectual belief or assent to the attitude of trust. In the Apostles' Creed we do not confess 'I believe that' but rather 'I believe in ...' There is a world of difference between 'that' and 'in.' There is a difference in saying 'I believe you are a human,' and 'I believe in you.' To believe in you means I put my trust in you. As Christians, we say we 'believe' in God, because our religion is essentially a relationship with God based on trust.

We Christians trust not only the promises of God and live accordingly, but we trust our very lives completely to God by surrender and commitment. We trust the everlasting arms of God, underneath us, to save us from fear, death, and hell. By faith we commit our lives into God's hands and we relax.

Action is Brokhoff's third 'A.'

By assent we said, 'I believe that;' by trust we said, 'I believe in.' But faith is more than assent and attitude; it is action, obedience, or works. Undoubtedly this is the most difficult dimension of faith.

A fact of life is that we do what we believe in. Faith precedes our actions. Because Columbus believed that the world was round, he set sail to go to India by going westward. Because the Nazis believed the Jews were a menace to society, there was a holocaust. Because we believe that Jesus is the Christ we will be baptized and join the church.

Belief and unbelief

The father of the demon-possessed boy believed. He assented to what he knew about Jesus. His attitude of trust was evident. He acted on his faith. The father brought his son to Jesus and declared, "I believe." Yet in the same breath he also cried out to Jesus, "Help my unbelief."

"I believe; help my unbelief" might seem a contradiction. However, only the existence of this father's faith could have made him conscious of its weakness. His request for Christ to help him overcome his unbelief showed his insight into the power of Christ to do far more than merely heal his child. Although it may have been dimmed by the disciples' failure, the father's faith revived and flourished when he stood face to face with Jesus. Addressing this still prevalent phenomenon William Barclay comments, "The Church may disappoint us; the servants of the Church may disappoint us; but when we battle our way face to face with Jesus Christ, he never disappoints us."

The father came to Jesus seeking help for his son. He quickly recognized the limitations of his own faith and thus realized that he needed help as well. The relationship of doubt and faith will be explored in Chapter 3. Here, however, this father's timeless supplication, "I believe; help my unbelief," helps to remind third millennium Christians what it is to confess our faltering and imperfect faith, using an ancient creed that begins with the words "I believe."

I believe

To say "I believe" is to give intellectual assent to the fundamental doctrines of the Christian faith: that God is our Father, the creator of the heavens and the earth; that Jesus is his only Son, our only Savior; that the ongoing ministry of the Holy Spirit makes us one with God and with each other.

To say "I believe" is also to give evidence of our attitude of trust, an attitude that says to God: I will step out in faith, trusting you to guide my steps; I will return good for evil, trusting your goodness and your mercy; I will follow your call through the lonely places, trusting the promise of your presence with me, now and in the life to come.

And finally, to say, "I believe" is to act. It is to weld our intellectual assent and our attitude of trust to faithful actions in our daily lives.

These elements of faith come together each time we confess the first words of the Apostles' Creed, "I believe."

For reflection and response
1. What do you mean when you say "I believe …?"
2. What is the difference between believing "from the top of the head" and believing "from the bottom of the heart?"
3. Have you ever said to God, "Help my unbelief?" If so, how has God answered that prayer?
4. What do you hope to gain from this study of the Apostles' Creed?

Pray and give God thanks for his desire to give abundantly to us and especially for his gift of faith. You may wish to pray Psalm 23 or to use that psalm as a model for your prayer.

Scripture passages for further study
II Chronicles 20:1-24; Habakkuk 2:1-4; John 6:25-29, John 20:30-31; Romans 10:14-17; Ephesians 6:13-17.

Additional resources
Diogenes Allen, *Christian Belief in a Postmodern World* (Louisville: Westminster/John Knox Press, 1989).

William Barclay, *The Gospel of Mark* (Philadelphia: Westminster, 1956).

John R. Brokhoff, *This You Can Believe: A New Look at the Apostles' Creed* (Lima, OH: C.S.S. Publishing, 1987).

Edward Dowey, *A Commentary on the Confession of 1967 and an Introduction to "The Book of Confessions"* (Philadelphia: The Westminster Press, n.d.).

2

THE FUNCTION
OF CREEDS

Suggested Scripture readings
Mark 8:27-30; Philippians 2:5-11

What does it mean for Christians to say "I believe?"

If we are merely mouthing words by rote when we recite the Apostles' Creed, the two little words at its beginning, "I believe," may never come to our conscious attention. They may be skimmed over as a perfunctory prelude to the really important words that follow, words like God, Jesus Christ, and resurrection.

However, pausing to consider these two words will help to lay a firm foundation for a comprehensive study of the Creed. Indeed, if we have ears to hear, the words "I believe" will direct our attention both to the nature and purpose of creeds and to the nature of our faith. In Chapter 1 we looked at the words "I believe" in the light of what they can teach us about the nature of faith. In this chapter we will focus on the history and use of Christian creeds.

A brief history

Our English word "creed" comes from the Latin *credo*, which means, "I believe." A creed is thus my statement of what it is that I believe. More technically, a creed is a concise, formal, and authorized statement of essential Christian doctrine.

The earliest Christian creed was spoken by Peter at Caesarea Philippi. In response to Jesus' question, "But who do you say that I am," Peter, inspired by the Holy Spirit, replied, "You are the Christ" (Mark 8:29). Writing to the Philippians some three decades later, Paul concluded his marvelous Hymn to Christ with what remains the foundational creed of Christianity, "Jesus Christ is Lord" (Phil. 2:11).

But after the last apostle had died, after the canon of Scripture had been closed, Christians began to sense a need for clear and succinct summaries of the basic doctrines of their faith. So they drew upon the language of Scripture to formulate brief statements of their core beliefs. The most prominent of such statements – the Apostles', Nicene, and Athanasian Creeds – we now call the ecumenical creeds. These are accepted (with some variations) by the Roman Catholic, Eastern Orthodox, and most Protestant churches. Perhaps the most widely used of the ecumenical creeds is the Apostles' Creed.

Although its author remains unknown, the Apostles' Creed seems to have originated in first-century Rome as part of the instructions given to those preparing for baptism. By the end of the second century, a standard form of the Creed had emerged, slightly shorter than the one we now use. The material existed in two forms, one a declaration "I believe in …" the other as a series of questions and answers. In the latter, an individual preparing for baptism stood in the water and was asked "Do you believe in God the Father Almighty?" The individual responded "I believe" and was immersed. This pattern was repeated with the articles concerning the Son and the Holy Spirit.

Over the next few centuries it continued to undergo some modifications, until in sixth- or seventh-century France the Apostles' Creed as we now know it attained its final form. In the Middle Ages, a pious legend grew that attributed each phrase to one of the apostles. But even though the true historical development of the Creed was demonstrated during the Renaissance, its simplicity and directness so clearly reflect apostolic teachings that the name has been retained.

While creeds and confessions are a significant part of our Reformed heritage, other Christian traditions make little if any use of such resources. For example, many Baptist churches prefer not to use creeds, rightly recognizing that any human formulations may be superimposed on Scripture and that creeds can become exceedingly complex and abstract. However, the Presbyterian Church (U.S.A.) *Book of Order* recognizes creeds and confessions to be "subordinate standards in the Church, subject to the authority of Jesus Christ, the word of God, as the Scriptures bear witness to him" (G-2.0200). Properly understood and employed, creeds and confessions can serve several useful functions in the life of the church.

A three-dimensional purpose

John Brokhoff asks, "Why bother with the Creeds? Why not let each Christian decide what to believe?" He answers, "The Creeds have at least a three-dimensional purpose: Definition, Defense, and Declaration."

Definition. The first purpose of the creeds, Brokhoff writes, "is to define the Christian faith. What does a Christian believe, or what should a person believe to be a Christian? Are your beliefs in harmony with the Scriptures and the church's teachings? ... As long as the Creeds are known, no Christian should ever be unable to tell or explain what he or she believes. It is all in the Creeds. Holding to the Creeds, a Christian can say 'This is what I believe. I know what I believe, and I know that what I believe is the absolute truth because it comes from the Bible.'"

Once we have learned the Apostles' Creed, we will always have an answer to questions such as "Well, what *do* you

To know the Apostles' Creed is to know that what you believe is within the boundaries of Scripture and the historic teachings of the Church.

Christians believe? What makes you any different from Moslems, Buddhists, or goddess-worshippers?" To know the Apostles' Creed is to know that what you believe lies within the boundaries of Scripture and the historic teachings of the church.

Defense is the second purpose of the Creed. Even before the last apostle had died, some within the church were attempting to redefine the faith to their own advantage. Several of Paul's letters, some written only two or three decades after Jesus' resurrection, include sections combatting false teachings. Since such heresies emerged within the first-century church, Christians should not be surprised, or unprepared, when distortions of the Christian message circulate within the contemporary church. And we should keep in mind that the knowledge of the Creed is a ready defense against false doctrine.

Brokhoff notes that when bank tellers are trained, they do not study or handle counterfeit bills. Neither do they listen to lectures denouncing counterfeiters. Rather, they handle real money, day after day after day, so that if they ever do come across a counterfeit bill, they recognize it at once. "It is the same with the Creed. When we know it thoroughly and use it regularly, we at once can tell when a heresy is proclaimed. The Creed is our defense. The Creed states the truth. Any idea that does not agree is counterfeit."

Declaration is our individual and corporate witness, to ourselves and to the world, of what it is that we believe. Brokhoff reminds us that "Before ascending to heaven, Jesus told the disciples that they were to be his witnesses to all the world. The third purpose of creeds fulfills this need to declare our faith. We use the creeds for a corporate witnessing before God and the world. It is a positive, fearless declaration of our Christian faith. When the devil and his cohorts hear Christians with one voice repeating the Creed, they tremble! The Creed is for every Christian to declare his or her faith throughout everyday life. Luther said that a Christian should confess the Apostles' Creed eight times daily."

When Christians gather for worship and together recite the Apostles' Creed, we declare that these are the essential articles of our faith. When Christians scatter to be the church in the world, we remember that Christ commanded his disciples to go into the whole world and make disciples of all nations. Our knowledge of the Creed enables us to sound a clarion call, one that rises above the confusing clamor of contemporary life, one that draws men and women in need of salvation to the person and work of Jesus Christ.

I believe

Each time we confess our faith by reciting the Apostles' Creed, we would do well to remember this three-dimensional purpose of Christian creeds: Definition, Defense, and Declaration. Once we have taken the time to consider carefully the nature and purpose of creeds, these dimensions can come to mind each and every time we say the first words of the Creed, "I believe."

For reflection and response

1. Why do so many Christians continue to make use of a Creed that dates back almost 2,000 years? Do you find its antiquity a comfort or that it makes the Creed irrelevant?

2. What are some benefits, and possible problems, with the use of creeds in the church?

3. In your own words, tell how the Apostles' Creed could help you with the definition, defense, and declaration of your faith in Jesus Christ.

Pray and give God thanks that he has given us the Bible and the creeds for our instruction. You may wish to pray Psalm 19:7-11 or to use those verses as the model for your prayer.

Scripture passages for further study
Psalm 19:1-6; Romans 10:6-11; I Peter 3:15-16.

Additional resources
John R. Brokhoff, *This You Can Believe: A New Look at the Apostles' Creed* (Lima, Ohio: C.S.S. Publishing, 1987).

J.N.D. Kelly, *Early Christian Doctrines* (London: A&C Black, 1977).

John H. Leith, *Basic Christian Doctrine* (Louisville: Westminster/John Knox Press, 1993).

Philip Schaff, *The Creeds of Christendom* (Grand Rapids: Baker, 1977 [reprint of 1877 edition]).

3

THE PLACE OF DOUBT

Suggested Scripture readings
Matthew 28:16-20; James 1:2-8

Must Christians believe without reservation every affirmation of the Apostles' Creed? Is it possible to trust Jesus Christ as Savior and Lord and yet be unsure about some things the Bible teaches? Does having doubts mean lacking faith? Indeed, is doubt the opposite of faith?

To answer such questions, we must consider not only what we believe, but how we believe.

'But some doubted'

One place to look for answers to such questions may seem unlikely – the introduction to the Great Commission. In Matthew 28:16-17 we learn that after Jesus' resurrection "the eleven disciples went to Galilee, to the mountain where Jesus had told them to go. When they saw him, they worshiped him; but some doubted."

I must admit that when I think of the Great Commission, the words "but some doubted" are not the first that come to mind. But, especially considering their context, these words are very comforting. Some of the disciples – who had spent three years of their lives with Jesus, who had heard with their own ears his prophecy of his impending death and resurrection – doubted even as Jesus stood right before them. They had heard that the tomb was empty, walked miles to meet with Jesus, saw him and began to worship him, yet even as they worshiped some doubted.

That some disciples simultaneously worshiped and doubted reassures us that absolute freedom from doubt is not a precondition to the worship of God. Rather, the disciples' conflicted response indicates that having doubts about things we do not fully understand is not ultimately incompatible with worshiping the one we know to be our Savior and Lord.

How can that be? One way of approaching this question is to distinguish between the content of our faith and the structure of our faith; between what we believe and how we believe.

Content vs. structure

For example, Christians do not believe that God may exist, but then again, he may not. Neither do we believe that Jesus may or may not be God Incarnate, the second person of the Trinity. Doubts about the existence of God or the deity of Christ are not a part of the content of Christian faith. Christians believe and teach that God does exist, and that our Lord and Savior Jesus Christ is his only begotten Son.

However, as finite, not to mention fallen, human beings, there are times when our faith may be shaken, when circumstances may lead us to question our most basic beliefs. Perhaps we have doubted God's providence because the forecast rain never came and our crops withered and died. Perhaps we have doubted God's love because of a painful situation in our family. Perhaps, because a fervent prayer seems to have gone unanswered, we have wondered whether the God we worship even exists.

Yet, despite our doubts, we continue to worship. And, despite our doubts, God accepts our adoration and praise.

That is because God knows that we are finite, fallen, fallible creatures whose hearts and minds, clouded as they are by sin, are prone to doubt. Yet God continues to love us just as we are.

Nowhere in Scripture does God condemn a believer who has doubts. Remember Gideon? He had serious doubts about leading the people into battle, so he laid out a fleece not once, but twice. God honored both requests (Judges 6:36-40). And when Thomas said "Unless I see … I will not believe," Jesus answered, "Put your finger here; see my hands. Reach out your hand and put it into my side. Stop doubting and believe" (John 20:24-29).

While doubt is nowhere commended as an attitude to cultivate, neither does Scripture teach that our doubts lead God to cease caring for us. God knows the frailty of our human nature, and he responds to our doubts as to our other weaknesses – with steadfast love.

'Double-souled'

Understanding doubt as part of the structure but not the content of our faith also gives us insight into James 1:2-8 where James teaches that when we ask God for wisdom we should "believe and not doubt," for the one who makes this request while doubting the one of whom it is made "is a double-minded man, unstable in all he does."

"Double-minded," literally "double-souled," is a word found nowhere in Greek literature prior to this occurrence, which suggests that James may have coined the term for this occasion. A double-souled person is one who prays to a God he does not believe to exist. He doubts God's existence but hedges his bets. His doubt is a part of the content of his faith.

In contrast, the kinds of doubts that trouble Christians are part of the structure of our faith; that is, they arise out of how, not what, we believe. The doubt James writes about is part of the content of belief, a fundamental doubt that the God being addressed even exists. That distinguishes the

God knows the frailty of our human nature, and he responds to our doubts as to our other weaknesses – with steadfast love.

---

doubts of Christians from those of "double-souled" individuals, those who pray to a God whose existence they do not affirm.

Faith in Jesus Christ does not mean living a life free from doubts any more than it means living a life free of suffering, trials, and temptations. It does mean that when doubts arise, we can prayerfully discuss them with God and ask him for wisdom. That kind of doubt, which arises when faith seeks understanding, means that Christians cannot be "double-souled," nor can they make requests of God while harboring the kind of doubt James describes.

I believe

The biblical evidence clearly shows that it is possible to be a faithful follower of Jesus Christ and to have honest doubts about aspects of your faith. If you fear expressing your doubts, remember Christianity has survived 2,000 years, often in the face of intense persecution. So it seems quite unlikely that the faith will crumble because you have asked a hard question. If you doubt that reality, look back at what Matthew tells us about the disciples.

Had the disciples lacked faith, they never would have gone from Jerusalem to Galilee to meet someone they had watched die on a cross. Had the disciples lacked faith, they would not have worshiped their living Lord. They went and they worshiped, but some doubted. Yet despite their doubts, these disciples recognized their risen Lord as God in human flesh, and they worshiped him.

As we saw in Chapter 2, the most basic creed of the Christian faith is "Jesus Christ is Lord." To be sure, that confession does not give full expression to the breadth and depth of what it is to be a Christian. But once an individual confesses Jesus Christ as Lord, he or she is ready to begin an exhilarating exploration of the mind of God, an exploration that can be aided by a careful study of the Apostles' Creed.

Will doubts arise along the way? Undoubtedly. For doubt is not the opposite of faith. Disbelief is the opposite of faith. Doubt is merely a part of how we believe, one manifestation (among many) of our sin-tainted nature. But like the disciples, despite our doubts, we must worship our risen Lord. And like them, we must then obey the command to "go and make disciples of all nations," secure in Jesus' promise that "surely I am with you, to the very end of the age" (Matt. 28:19-20).

For reflection and response

1. In your own words, explain the difference between doubt as a part of what we believe and doubt as a part of how we believe.
2. What is the place of doubt in Christian faith and life?
3. Why is disbelief, not doubt, the opposite of faith?

Pray and give God thanks for remaining faithful when we are troubled by doubts. You may wish to pray Psalm 139:1-12 or to use those verses as a model for your prayer.

Scripture passages for further study

Genesis 15:1-15; Judges 6:34-40; Matthew 11:1-6; Mark 5:35-41; John 20:24-29.

Additional resources

Os Guiness, *Doubt: Faith in Two Minds* (Tring: Lion, 1979).

Alister McGrath, *The Sunnier Side of Doubt* (Grand Rapids: Zondervan, 1990).

Paul Tillich, *Dynamics of Faith: Faith and Belief: What They Are and What They Are Not* (New York: Harper & Brothers, 1957).

4

THE DOCTRINE
OF GOD

Suggested Scripture readings
Exodus 3:1-15; Revelation 4:1-11

Each time we recite the Apostles' Creed we begin, "I believe in God." But what do we personally know of the nature and character of God? How do we describe the One in whom we say we believe? Where do we begin when non-Christians ask us to tell them about our God?

We must begin by acknowledging that God is not subject to human definition, for "to define" is literally "to set the limits of." However, the suggested Scripture readings offer four parallels and one paradox that lead us toward a fuller understanding of the One of whom we say "I believe."

God reveals himself

Despite their vastly different situations, Moses and John encounter God in a similar way. Moses hears a voice from the burning bush calling him by name. John, as he sees the door in heaven, hears a voice like a trumpet calling "Come up here." From these encounters we learn that it is God who initiates the relationship between himself and his human creation.

Unlike many gods of ancient mythology, our God does not hide himself then punish human beings for failing to find and appease him. Instead, our God is a God who calls and invites, who encourages us to look and listen for his presence in our lives. From Genesis to Revelation, the Bible describes a God who is the same at the end as he was at the beginning, a God who never changes, a God who initiates a relationship with us by choosing to reveal himself.

God's call requires our response

God's self-revelation is simultaneously a call for a response. Moses' response is recorded, "Here I am." John's assent becomes evident as his next statement declares, "At once I was in the Spirit."

Such responses to God's call are characteristic of God's most faithful servants. Remember young Samuel? When Eli, the experienced priest, finally recognized that it was God calling Samuel, he taught Samuel the proper response. The boy went back to his bed and "The Lord came and stood there, calling as at other times 'Samuel! Samuel!' Then Samuel said, 'Speak, for your servant is listening'" (I Sam. 3:10).

Perhaps the most familiar call and response is found in Isaiah 6, where Isaiah sees a vision of heaven much like that which John describes. After being overwhelmed by God's greatness and his own sinfulness Isaiah writes, "Then I heard the voice of the Lord saying, 'Whom shall I send? And who will go for us?' And I said, 'Hear am I. Send me'" (Isa. 6:8).

Today God rarely appears at the foot of our bed, through a burning bush, or in an awe-inspiring highly-detailed vision of heaven. But then that never was God's usual way of revealing himself. Elijah experienced God's presence as a still, small voice. The Ethiopian eunuch heard God's call while sitting in a chariot reading a passage of Scripture that he did not fully understand. It is still with a quiet voice, often as we meditate on Scripture, that God reveals himself to most of us today. And the most appropriate response remains, "Hear I am. Speak Lord."

"The perfect knowledge of God is so to know him that we are sure we must not be ignorant of him, yet we cannot describe him. We must believe, must apprehend, must worship; and such acts of devotion must stand in lieu of definition."

— Hilary of Poitiers

God is light

Moses hears God speaking from fire. John writes that the one who sat on the heavenly throne "had the appearance of jasper and carnelian." What jasper and carnelian have in common with fire is their concentration of light.

Paul describes God as the One "who lives in unapproachable light, whom no one has seen or can see" (I Tim. 6:16). And in these parallel encounters, neither Moses nor John comes into unmediated contact with Almighty God. Our own experience confirms that we cannot stand very close to a raging fire. Neither can we look for long into a brilliant light. Without external aids, such as asbestos suits or darkened glasses, human beings are simply unable to withstand such intensities. Similarly, no sinful human being can stand unaided in the presence of God.

One reason that fire and light are among the most frequent biblical metaphors for God is that our fallen nature prevents us from drawing near to the unapproachable light of God. Just as our sin prevents us from making the first move toward God, so it prevents us from coming into the presence of God apart from our Mediator, Jesus Christ.

God is holy

God tells Moses, "Take off your sandals, for the place where you are standing is holy ground," and in John's vision six-winged creatures hover around the throne where they never stop saying, "Holy, holy, holy is the Lord God Almighty."

The Hebrew word for holy, *qadosh*, seems to derive from two roots, one meaning "to cut, to separate," the other meaning "to be clean, pure, consecrated." The ancient Israelites applied this adjective to their priests, as those separated out and consecrated to the service of God, and also to themselves as a people called apart by God especially for service to God.

When "holy" is used to describe God, it refers to that which is in the realm of the sacred as opposed to the common or profane. It connotes that which is totally good and entirely without evil. As Thomas E. McComiskey observes:

> God is intrinsically holy, and he calls his people to be holy, providing for them the standards of obedience whereby that holiness may be maintained. Because God is holy, he is free from the moral imperfections and frailties common to man and can be counted on to be faithful to his promises. ... It is unthinkable that a holy God could condone sin; such a concept would involve a diffusion of the sacred and profane, thus destroying the nature of holiness.

To be in God's presence is to be in a holy place, a place where evil and faithlessness cannot exist. As God is holy, so God's people are to be holy.

A paradox

In addition to these four parallels, one dissimilarity between these texts is striking. God speaks directly to Moses and reveals to him his name, "Yahweh." It is from a distance that John sees God sitting in awesome splendor on his heavenly throne and hears God's attributes declared by other beings. In theological terms, the difference between Moses' experience and John's is the difference between God's immanence and God's transcendence.

To say that God is immanent is to say that God is as near

to us as our own thoughts, as close to us as our own feelings. It is to say that God himself is his gift to us. However, God is equally transcendent, that is, inconceivably above us and beyond us. God in his existence and essence is so far removed from our human condition that our limited senses are unable to perceive him, let alone to define his character and nature.

The paradox is that God is simultaneously immanent and transcendent. God is in us as we live and move and have our being within him. God is also reigning on the throne of heaven, exercising his might and majesty in ways we cannot begin to comprehend. Hilary of Poitiers, a fourth-century theologian from Gaul, acknowledged that reality when he wrote:

> Let us confess by our silence that words cannot describe [God]; let sense admit that it is foiled in the attempt to apprehend, and reason in the effort to define. I am well aware that no words are adequate to describe his attributes ... the best combination of words we can devise cannot indicate the reality and the greatness of God. The perfect knowledge of God is so to know him that we are sure we must not be ignorant of him, yet we cannot describe him. We must believe, must apprehend, must worship; and such acts of devotion must stand in lieu of definition.

Doubtless Moses and John would have agreed with Hilary's assessment. We too can share this perception of God's greatness and this apprehension of God's presence as in our worship we confess, "I believe in God."

For reflection and response

1. Why must God reveal himself to us if we are to know him?
2. What does it mean to say that God is "holy?" What does it mean to say that God's people are "holy?"
3. How is it possible for God to be simultaneously immanent and transcendent?

Pray and give God thanks for his incomparable nature and for choosing to reveal himself to us. You may wish to pray

Psalm 97 or to use that psalm as a model for your prayer.

Scripture passages for further study

I Samuel 3:1-11; Isaiah 6:1-8; Acts 8:26-40; I Corinthians 2:9-10; I Timothy 6:13-16; I Peter 1:13-16; I John 1:5.

Additional resources

Thomas E. McComiskey, "*qadosh*" in *Theological Wordbook of the Old Testament* (Chicago: Moody Press, 1980).

Rudolph Otto, *The Idea of the Holy* (Oxford: Oxford University Press, 1923).

J.I. Packer, *Knowing God* (Downers Grove: InterVarsity Press, 1973).

J.B. Phillips, *Your God Is Too Small* (New York: Macmillan, 1954).

Robert Sokolowski, *The God of Faith and Reason* (Notre Dame: University of Notre Dame Press, 1982).

5

GOD THE FATHER

Suggested Scripture reading
John 5:16-23

What's in a name?

Family names often trace back to one of four sources: First, there are names that identify a trait or characteristic, such as Swift or Strong. A second source of surnames deals with location. Which John do you mean? John Atwater or John Overbrook. A third common source derives from occupations: Foreman, Taylor, Miller. A fourth source was to identify children by their father's name. John's son thus became Johnson, similarly Robinson and Anderson.

Names enable us to identify individuals. They help us to distinguish one individual from another. Merely by mentioning a person's name we can bring to mind such diverse aspects as physical appearance, outstanding qualities or abilities, and the impact of that person on our lives. And what is true about the names of people is even more true of the names of God.

The Apostles' Creed refers to God as "Father" and "Almighty." Since each name deserves careful attention, this chapter will focus on God as Father, while the next will consider the designation God Almighty.

Jesus calls God 'Father'

The opening verses of John 5 describe Jesus' healing of a man who had been an invalid for 38 years. That this healing took place on the Sabbath aroused the anger of certain Jewish religious leaders. Calling God "Father" angered them even more. "For this reason the Jews tried all the harder to kill him; not only was he breaking the Sabbath, but he was even calling God his own Father, making himself equal with God" (John 5:17-18).

Only 15 times in the Old Testament is God called "Father," and in every instance God is spoken of as the Father of the nation of Israel, never as the Father of an individual Israelite. However, 170 times in the gospels Jesus speaks of, or to, God as "Father," in Aramaic *abba*. *Abba*, which might also be translated "Daddy," is a term of endearment less formal than "Father," a form of address that may be freely used by toddlers yet used without embarrassment by adult children. The personal nature of *abba* is shown by the fact that slaves were not permitted to use the term when addressing the head of a family.

Jesus answers the Jewish objections to his healing on the Sabbath by specifically and insistently referring to God as his Father, and to himself as God's Son. For the Jews of Jesus' day, who would not even pronounce the name of God, this was blasphemy. But for Jesus, this Father-Son relationship was at the heart of his earthly life and ministry.

As the Lutheran theologian Wolfhart Pannenberg observes, Father "was the only name for God Jesus used. ... Therefore, the exchange of this name inevitably results in turning to another God."

Denying God as Father

Despite Pannenberg's insightful assessment, attempts have been made in some segments of the church to exclude from Christian worship all references to God as "Father." Some

Paul kneels before God as his Father because it is from God that 'all fatherhood in heaven and on earth derives its name.'

endeavors are extreme examples of oversimplification, such as Mary Daly's overworked aphorism, "If God is male then the male is God." Of course, no orthodox Christian theologian has ever ascribed male gender to God. Neither does historic Christianity teach that men (or women) are divine.

As Aida Besançon Spencer writes:

> God is Father not because God is masculine. God is Father because 'father' in the ancient world was a helpful metaphor to communicate certain aspects of God's character. God is Spirit, neither male nor female. God has no form at all (as God clearly revealed to Moses in Deut. 4:15-16). Therefore many metaphors and similes, actions, and descriptive adjectives are needed to help us understand God.

Other efforts to force Christians to abandon the biblical and creedal language of "God the Father" are dangerous and deceptive because they contain bits of truth. One such argument is that Christians should not refer to God as "Father" because the word "Father" is insufficient to convey the entire reality of the relationship between God and humankind.

It is true that no single name (nor indeed the whole of human language) can completely express the reality of God. However, it is not valid, logically or theologically, to leap from this truth to the claim that Christians must not use the name "Father" because that name cannot convey all that can be known of God. The whole truth is that Scripture and the Confessions understand and express the reality that "Father" is not the only name by which God is known.

Those who insist that Christians never use the biblical,

creedal language of God as Father deny themselves, and would deny us all, irreplaceable insight into the nature and character of God as God has revealed himself to us. Indeed, those who would force Christians to renounce the biblical teaching of God as "Father" – on the grounds that calling God "Father" is a flawed attempt to apply to our own human experience of fatherhood to a God who is beyond all human understanding – get the reality of God as Father exactly backwards.

God the source of fatherhood

When Paul writes, "For this reason I kneel before the Father, from whom all fatherhood in heaven and on earth derives its name" (Eph. 3:14-15), the direction of the attribution is essential: Paul kneels before God as his Father because *it is from God* that *"all fatherhood ... derives its name."*

That means the name "God the Father" is *not* a human attempt to make God in man's image. Neither is God called "Father" on the basis of a distorted human analogy. Rather, fatherhood is an innate, inherent, uncreated aspect of the nature of God. Consequently, to address God as "Father" is not to engage in sexist rhetoric, nor is it to settle for a purely human linguistic construction. It is to address God using one of the names by which God revealed himself to us, the name we were taught by Jesus.

Certainly the relationship between Christ the Son and God the Father was unique. Nevertheless, it is not completely unconnected to the father-child relationship God maintains with each of us. For Jesus taught his disciples to call God *abba* (Matt. 6:9), a term that conveys the intimacy and familiarity of the father-child relationship.

Jesus called God "Father," and thereby offended certain Jews. Jesus taught his disciples to call God "our Father," and his disciples were persecuted as he was. So it is not surprising, although it is sad, that even within the Church today there are some who choose to take offense at those who continue to use the language of Scripture and to say, "I believe in God the Father."

I believe in God the Father

To say, "I believe in God the Father" is to declare, to one another and to the world, that there is Someone who cares for every individual as an ideal father would and should. It is to say that there is a transcendent God in heaven who desires a Father-child relationship with each of his human creations. It is to say that this Father so loved the world that he sent his only Son to live with us and within us; that whoever believes in him should not perish but have eternal life.

Through Jesus and the Scriptures, God has revealed himself to us as Father. Our response to that gracious revelation can only be to say, "I believe in God the Father."

For reflection and response

1. What might cause people today to shy away from calling God "Father?"

2. If you were privileged to have a loving father, what is the most loving thing you remember your father doing for you? If not, what did you especially wish your father would have done for you?

3. What does Jesus' reference to God as "Father" reveal about the nature of Jesus' relationship with God? What does it reveal about our relationship with God?

Pray and give God thanks for being our perfect Father. You may wish to pray the Lord's Prayer (Matt. 6:9-13) or to use those verses as a model for your prayer.

Scripture passages for further study

Deuteronomy 4:15-16; Psalm 68:4-6; Isaiah 64:8; Matthew 7:9-11; John 14:5-14; Romans 8:12-17; Ephesians 3:14-15.

Additional resources

Elizabeth Achtemeier, "Why God is not Mother," *Christianity Today* (August 16, 1993, pp. 16-23).

Donald D. Hook and Alvin F. Kimel Jr., "Calling God 'Father:' A Theolinguistic Analysis," *Faith and Philosophy* (Vol. 12, No. 2, April 1995).

Wolfhart Pannenberg, *An Introduction to Systematic Theology* (Grand Rapids: Eerdmans, 1991).

Aida Besançon Spencer, "Father-Ruler: The Meaning of the Metaphor 'Father' for God in the Bible," *Journal of the Evangelical Theological Society* (Vol. 39, No. 3, September 1996).

6

GOD ALMIGHTY

Suggested Scripture reading
Genesis 17:1-8

Each time we recite the Apostles' Creed we confess our faith in "God the Father Almighty." In Chapter 5 we considered the importance of names. In particular we looked at God's revelation of himself as Father, and saw that that name revealed fatherhood to be an innate aspect of God's nature. In this chapter we will consider what it means that God reveals himself as *el-shaddai*, God Almighty.

God's self-revelation

God first reveals himself by this name to Abram 24 years after promising, "I will make you a great nation" (Gen. 12:2). Now, "When Abram was ninety-nine years old, the Lord appeared to him and said, 'I am God Almighty [*el-shaddai*]; walk before me and be blameless. ... this is my covenant with you: You will be the father of many nations. No longer will you be called Abram; your name will be Abraham, for I have made you a father of many nations'" (Gen. 17:1, 4-5).

God's revelation of himself, in particular God's announcing his own name, is always an act of immense significance. In Abram's day, some 1,800 years before the birth of Christ, most people considered human life to be completely surrounded by invisible divine forces, good and evil spirits that had to be discovered and appeased, lest by inattention to some god or gods, helpless humans anger the capricious deities into causing sickness, famine, or flood.

As Abram's spiritual descendants, contemporary Christians should not overlook the dramatic and decisive nature of this self-revelation. For once God revealed his name to Abram and established a covenant with him, Abram, and through him all people, no longer had to fear giving inadvertent offense to an unknown deity. Abram received from God a legally binding set of duties and obligations that God himself had promised to fulfill. And, in giving him his name, *el-shaddai* gave Abram essential information about the nature and the character of the One who had promised to remain faithful not only to Abram, but to his descendants throughout all generations.

El-shaddai

El-shaddai is a compound name. *El* is the Hebrew equivalent for our English word "god." It can be translated with a lower case "g" to indicate a god or gods in general, or with an upper case "G" to identify or address the God of Abram. *El* conveys a sense of might and power, as in Psalm 77:14, "You are the God [*el*] who performs miracles; you display your power among the peoples."

The derivation of *shaddai* is less certain. Traditionally, Old Testament scholars have traced *shaddai* back to a Hebrew root-word meaning "strong," "powerful," or "violent." From this perspective, *el-shaddai* is seen as the God who reveals himself by special deeds of power, particularly those deeds in which nature acts contrary to its norm. This was the understanding of the Greek translation of the Old Testament, which uses *pantokrator*, "all-powerful," and of Jerome, whose use of *omnipotens* in his fourth-century translation of the Bible into Latin has influenced English translations of Scripture from the King James Version to the present.

Some more recent interpreters trace *shaddai* to the Hebrew

*"To experience God's fullness one must empty self.
The less empty of self we are, the less of blessing
God can pour into us."*

— *Nathan Stone*

word for "breast," and suggest that a better translation of *el-shaddai* is "the all-sufficient God," that is, the God who gives life, the God who sustains life, the God who blesses, nourishes, nurtures, and comforts. Certainly this is the sense conveyed by *shaddai* in the blessing given by Jacob, Abraham's grandson, to his own son Joseph:

"Joseph is a fruitful vine, a fruitful vine near a spring ... because of your father's god [*el*] who helps you, because of the Almighty [*shaddai*] who blesses you with the blessings of the heavens above, blessings of the deep that lies below, blessings of the breast and womb" (Gen. 49:22, 25). Isaiah often used similar imagery, perhaps nowhere more beautifully than in his closing chapters where he writes of God giving birth to and nursing his people until they "delight in his overflowing abundance" (Isa. 66:11).

God revealed himself to Abram and then instructed him to "walk before me and be blameless." The sequence is significant. God did not come to Abram and say "If you walk before me and are blameless, then and only then will I reveal my name and supply your needs." Rather, Abram's blameless (from a root meaning "complete") walk before God was to be his response to God's gracious self-revelation as *el-shaddai*.

God alone is all-sufficient

To Abram – who at God's calling left a settled homeland, comfortable circumstances, family, and friends to go on a long, possibly dangerous journey to a land he did not know –

God promised land, an incalculable number of descendants, and a spiritual mission. Abram had lived three quarters of a century when those promises first were made, and he waited nearly a quarter-century more for them to be fulfilled.

It was in his own time that the all-sufficient God, the God who makes fruitful, fulfilled the promise he had made decades before. And as he reaffirmed his intention to supply all he had promised, God also changed Abram's name from "exalted father" to Abraham, "father of a multitude." Abraham learned that what God promises, only God can deliver. He learned that, in and of himself, he was not sufficient. He learned that God alone is *el-shaddai*.

Many Christians still need to learn that lesson. Some of us need to be taught more than once. We all need to recognize and admit our own insufficiency before we can experience the all-sufficiency of God. Of this important truth Nathan Stone writes:

> To experience God's fullness one must empty self. It is not easy to empty self. It was never easy to do that. The less empty of self we are, the less of blessing God can pour into us; the more of pride and self-sufficience, the less fruit we can bear. Sometimes only chastening can make us realize this.

> The same *el-shaddai* of the Old Testament is the One who in the New chastens whom he loves that, being exercised thereby, they may yield the peaceable fruit of holiness or righteousness. He is the same One who has chosen us to bring forth fruit, much fruit, and that this fruit should remain. As the all-sufficient One he says, 'Apart from me you can do nothing.'

God Almighty

It is especially appropriate for Christians in the third Christian millennium to confess their belief in God as *el-shaddai*. For we must deal with New Age ideologies that believe and teach that human life is surrounded by unseen and unknown cosmic forces that human beings must discover, get in touch with, and somehow placate. (Such modern innovations are, of course, merely the most recent revivals of pagan beliefs that existed at least as early as Abram.) Christians can, indeed must, respond to such assertions by proclaiming God as *el-shaddai*, the One who alone is able to supply every human need, above all the inescapable human need to be in personal relationship with God.

When we confess our faith by reciting the Apostles' Creed, we remind ourselves, and announce to the world, that the One in whom we believe is the almighty, all-sufficient God, the God who creates, nurtures, establishes, sustains, protects, and blesses us. Our own insufficiency, and the all-sufficiency of God, should come to mind each time we say, "I believe in *God* the Father *Almighty*."

For reflection and response

1. In what ways has God shown you that he is sufficient to supply your needs?
2. What difference does it make in daily life to know that God can supply all your needs?
3. How can affirming our belief in God as *el-shaddai* help Christians respond to New Age assertions that we are surrounded by cosmic forces that must be discovered and appeased?

Pray and give God thanks for being able and willing to supply all our needs. You may wish to pray Psalm 91 or to use that psalm as a model for your prayer.

Scripture passages for further study

Genesis 49:22-26; Exodus 3:1-15; Psalm 67:1-7; Isaiah 66:10-13; John 15:1-8; Revelation 19:1-6.

Additional resources

Russell Chandler, *Understanding the New Age* (Grand

Rapids: Zondervan, 1993).

Victor P. Hamilton, "*shaddai*," in *Theological Wordbook of the Old Testament* (Chicago: Moody Press, 1980).

Christopher B. Kaiser, *The Doctrine of God* (Westchester, Ill: Crossway Books, 1982).

Nathan J. Stone, *Names of God* (Chicago: Moody Press, 1944).

7

MAKER OF HEAVEN AND EARTH

Suggested Scripture readings
Genesis 1:1-23; Romans 8:18-25, 38-39

In *Maker of Heaven and Earth: The Christian Doctrine of Creation in the Light of Modern Knowledge,* Langdon Gilkey writes:

> The idea that God is the Creator of all things is the indispensable foundation on which the other beliefs of the Christian faith are based. It affirms what the Christian believes about the status of God in the whole realm of reality: He is the Creator of everything else. On this affirmation logically depends all that Christians say about God, about the world they live in, and about their own history, destiny, and hope. The most fundamental question of religious thought is: who is God – He in whom we put our trust? And the primary answer in both Bible and creed is: 'He is the maker of the heavens and the earth.'

More recently, Wolfhart Pannenberg has observed that "the doctrine of creation in all its parts serves as a consolidation and corroboration of belief in God. ... In traditional theological terminology, the doctrine of creation does not relate only to creation, but also to conservation, redemption, and eschatology; in other words, to the entire economy of God's action."

Creation in Scripture

From Genesis through Revelation, Scripture speaks of the creative activity of God.

The very first words of the Bible, "In the beginning, God created the heavens and the earth," acknowledge God to be the One who brought into being everything other than himself.

Two different Hebrew verbs may be translated "create." *Yasar* emphasizes the creation of an object. This is the sense in which human beings "create" such things as dinners and dining room tables. However, the word used in Genesis 1:1 is *bara*, which emphasizes the initiation of an object. Throughout the Old Testament, *bara* in this grammatical form refers exclusively to God's creative activity. Thus Genesis points beyond human ability to that which only God can accomplish.

Isaiah declares, "This is what the Lord says – your Redeemer, who formed you in the womb: I am the Lord, who has made all things, who alone stretched out the heavens, who spread out the earth by myself" (Isa. 44:24). Jeremiah adds, "But God made the earth by his power; he founded the world by his wisdom and stretched out the heavens by his understanding" (Jer. 10:12).

In the New Testament, John's gospel opens with an echo of Genesis, "In the beginning was the Word, and the Word was with God, and the Word was God. He was with God in the beginning. Through him all things were made; without him nothing was made that has been made" (John 1:1-3). The word order of the first sentence places the emphasis on "In the beginning." And the Greek *arche*, here translated "beginning," often connotes "origin," which seems to be John's intent.

Finally, in Revelation 4:11 the 24 elders gathered around God's throne sing, "You are worthy, our Lord and God, to receive glory and honor and power, for you created all things, and by your will they were created and have their being."

*"In traditional theological terminology, the doc-
trine of creation does not relate only to creation,
but also to conservation, redemption, and eschatology; in other words, to the entire economy of
God's action."*

— Wolfhart Pannenberg

Creation and science

Paul writes, "I consider that our present sufferings are not
worth comparing with the glory that will be revealed in us"
(Rom. 8:18).

The word here translated "I consider" is *logizomai*, from
which we get our English word "logic." The Greek connotes
"a firm conviction reached by rational thought on the basis of
the gospel." Paul's choice of this word in this context reminds
us that faith and reason are not antagonists. Rather, they com-
plement each other.

Like Paul, third millennium Christians can be guided by
the gospel as we use our minds to explore all that God has
created. Living in an age when some would substitute modern
science for Christian faith as the ultimate foundation of
human hope and meaning, we can freely use our God-given
minds to pursue a biblical understanding of creation, which in
turn will draw us toward the One who created out of nothing
all that now exists.

Of the validity and importance of this historic Christian
doctrine of *creatio ex nihilo* John Polkinghorne, a theoretical
physicist and Anglican priest, writes, "The doctrine safe-
guards the fundamental theological intuition that creation is
separate from its Creator, that he has made ontological room
for something other than himself." The biblical doctrine of
creation thus counters such presently popular distortions as
process theology and pantheism.

Creation's limits

Paul concludes his reflection on creation, and the Creator's love, with the moving testimony, "For I am convinced that neither death nor life, neither angels nor demons, neither the present nor the future, nor any powers, neither height nor depth, nor anything else in all creation, will be able to separate us from the love of God that is in Christ Jesus our Lord" (Rom. 8:38-39).

Paul Achtemeier comments:

No dimension of reality one can imagine has the power to frustrate God's care and love for us. What Paul is listing are categories of creation – natural and supernatural – which in his understanding of the world could be candidates for exercising power over us. No creation, not even time or space, can ever separate the Creator from those whom he loves. What Paul means by such a statement is the assurance that there is no other power than God's which can affect our final destiny.

And Langdon Gilkey observes:

Without the idea of God's creation of the world, of history, and of man, the Gospel of the redemption of man's life from sin becomes meaningless, self-contradictory, and vain. The idea of creation expresses that fundamental relation between God and the world within which the Gospel of redemption is both important and viable, and so this conception provides the indispensable framework within which the Christian faith speaks its message of love.

Maker of heaven and earth

To confess God as "maker of heaven and earth" is to affirm, to ourselves and to all who will listen, that our God is the God who made us and the world in which we live. It is to confess that God is sovereign over time and space; famines, fires, and floods; things visible and invisible.

At the same time, to say that we believe in God as the maker of heaven and earth is to confess our hope in the salvation God has promised to all who believe. It is to say that we have already been adopted as God's children, that our redemption is a present reality, and that we will experience the full measure of our salvation when God's purpose for all creation is at last fulfilled.

Finally, to confess that we believe in God the Father Almighty, maker of heaven and earth, is to acknowledge that nothing in all creation can separate us from his love. No matter what our circumstances, or how they change; no matter what our physical, mental, or emotional condition; no matter what modern science may discover or modern theologians try to teach; the God who made heaven and earth has chosen us to be his people. And because the one who chose us is also the one who made us, nothing can ever separate us from his love.

May God recall to our hearts and minds these indispensable, fundamental realities each time we confess our belief in God as "maker of heaven and earth."

For reflection and response

1. What can creation tell us about the Creator? When have you been especially drawn toward the Creator by experiencing the creation?

2. What important things can creation not tell us about the Creator? What is needed to keep us from worshipping creation rather than the Creator?

3. How does the biblical teaching that God is the maker of heaven and earth protect us from false teachings and free us to sing God's praises?

Pray and give God thanks for being the maker of heaven and earth. You may wish to pray Psalm 148 or to use that psalm as a model for your prayer.

Scripture passages for further study

Psalm 102:25-27; Psalm 104:24-30; Psalm 139:7-16; Jeremiah 10:6-16; John 1:1-3; Colossians 1:15-17; Revelation 4:1-11.

Additional resources

Paul Achtemeier, *Romans* (Atlanta: John Knox Press, 1985).

Langdon Gilkey, *Maker of Heaven and Earth: The Christian Doctrine of Creation in the Light of Modern Knowledge* (Garden City, NY: Doubleday, 1959).

Wolfhart Pannenberg, *An Introduction to Systematic Theology* (Grand Rapids: Eerdmans, 1991).

John Polkinghorne, *The Faith of a Physicist: Reflections of a Bottom-Up Thinker* (Princeton: Princeton University Press, 1994).

Hugh Ross, *Creation and Time* (Colorado Springs: NavPress, 1994).

8

THE HUMANITY
OF JESUS

Suggested Scripture readings
John 1:1-4, 14; Philippians 2:5-11; I John 4:1-6

If we could directly perceive God through our five physical senses, what would God look like? What would God sound like? And, most important, how would we respond to this God whom we were able to see and hear?

J.B. Phillips, in his classic devotional study *Your God is Too Small*, takes an illuminating approach to such questions, writing:

> It is a fascinating problem for us human beings to consider how the Eternal Being – wishing to show men His own Character focused, His own Thought expressed, and His own Purpose demonstrated – could introduce Himself into the stream of human history without disturbing or disrupting it. There must obviously be an almost unbelievable 'scaling down' of the 'size' of God to match the life of the planet. There must be a complete acceptance of the space-and-time limitations of this present life. The thing must be done properly – it must not, for example, be merely an act put on for man's benefit. If it is to be done at all God must *be* man.

Historic Christianity has always and everywhere acknowledged that God did become human in Jesus Christ; that Jesus Christ was simultaneously fully human and fully divine, God Incarnate. With the phrase of the Apostles' Creed "I believe in

... Jesus Christ, [God's] only Son, our Lord" we begin a study of the theological discipline known as christology, the doctrines of the person and work of Jesus Christ.

While the classic formulations of christological doctrines are found in the Nicene Creed and Chalcedonian Definition, considerable attention is once again being focused on christology. Such public attention reminds us that as Christianity begins its third millennium it is imperative for all Christians to know what we believe about Jesus and why. For christological controversies have often provoked defining moments in the history of the church.

As we begin our exploration of christology, this chapter will consider Jesus' full and necessary humanity. This focus must not obscure an equal emphasis on his full deity, which will be the subject of Chapter 9.

Jesus' full humanity

Daniel Migliore writes:

> Jesus is *fully human*. While the New Testament does not give us materials for a biography of Jesus, there can be no doubt that it refers to a concrete human being who is like us in all respects, except in that alienation from and hostility to the grace of God which is the essence of sin. ... it is a complete distortion of the humanity of Jesus as depicted in the gospel story to claim that maleness is an ontological necessity of the incarnation of the Word of God.

The New Testament includes numerous references to Jesus' physical, mental, and emotional conditions. Physically, Jesus was born as a human baby and grew through childhood into adulthood just as other children grow (Luke 2:7, 40). He became tired (John 4:6), hungry (Matt. 4:2), and thirsty (John 19:28). As Wayne Grudem observes,

> The culmination of Jesus' human limitations in terms of his human body is seen when he died on the cross. His human body ceased to have life in it and ceased to function, just as ours does when we die.

> *"Jesus is* fully human. *While the New Testament does not give us materials for a biography of Jesus, there can be no doubt that it refers to a concrete human being who is like us in all respects, except in that alienation from and hostility to the grace of God which is the essence of sin."*
> — Daniel Migliore

Jesus also experienced and expressed a range of human emotion. When John writes of Jesus' soul and spirit being "troubled" (John 12:27, 13:21), he chooses a Greek word often used of people when they are anxious or surprised by danger. Jesus "marveled" at the faith of the centurion (Matt. 8:10) and "wept" at the death of his friend Lazarus (John 11:35). The author of Hebrews assures us that the human Jesus was "one who has been tempted in every way, just as we are – yet was without sin" (Heb. 4:15). That Jesus faced genuine temptation means that he had a genuine human nature, "For God cannot be tempted by evil" (James 1:13).

The theological term used to describe God the Son becoming human is *incarnation*, from the Latin *incarnare*, "to make flesh." Incarnation is not a conversion of deity into humanity but rather the assumption of humanity into God. Countless books and articles have been written in vain attempts to explain how the incarnation took place. How the Word became flesh is beyond human comprehension. The more important question, "Why?", is succinctly answered by John Calvin, "The sole purpose of Christ's incarnation was our redemption" (*Institutes*, 2.12.2).

Jesus' necessary humanity

Many inadequate or inaccurate explanations of the incarnation have been offered throughout church history. The earliest

Christians had to confront a false teaching known as "docetism," from the Greek word meaning "to seem" or "to appear." Docetists taught that Jesus was not really human, but only seemed, or appeared, to be a man. Underlying this heresy was the assumption that material creation is inherently evil, and that therefore the Son of God could not have become truly human.

This teaching was clearly refuted by John when he wrote:

> This is how you can recognize the Spirit of God: Every spirit that acknowledges that Jesus Christ has come in the flesh is from God, but every spirit that does not acknowledge Jesus is not from God. This is the spirit of the antichrist, which you have heard is coming; and even now is already in the world (I John 4:2-3).

Grudem offers an important word of warning when he reminds us that "Modern evangelicals who neglect to teach on the full humanity of Christ can unwittingly support docetic tendencies in their hearers." He also lists several reasons "why Jesus had to be fully man if he was going to be the Messiah."

One reason is that Jesus' full humanity is necessary for him to be our example and pattern. John tells us, "whoever claims to live in him must walk as Jesus did" (I John 2:6), while Paul assures us that as Christians we are continually "being transformed into his likeness with ever-increasing glory" (II Cor. 3:18). Throughout our Christian lives we are to "fix our eyes on Jesus the author and perfecter of our faith" (Heb. 12:2). Paul teaches that Jesus is also our example in death (Phil. 3:10). Grudem comments, "Our goal should be to be like Christ all our days, up to the point of death, and to die with unfailing obedience to God, with strong trust in him, and with love and forgiveness to others."

But perhaps most important, Jesus' full humanity is necessary because sin has alienated humanity from God; therefore, we need a mediator who can fully represent us to God and fully represent God to us. Paul taught that only one person ever fulfilled this requirement: "For there is one God and one mediator between God and men, the man Christ Jesus" (I Tim. 2:5).

In the famous phrase of Gregory of Nazianzus, the full humanity of Jesus Christ is required because "That which he has not assumed, he has not healed."

Our response

J.B. Phillips writes of the Incarnation of God in Jesus of Nazareth, of the Eternal Word becoming fully human:

> If for one moment we imagine the claim to be true the mind almost reels at its significance. It can only mean that here is Truth, here is the Character of God, the true Design for life, the authentic Yardstick of values, the reliable confirming or correcting of all gropings and inklings about Beauty, Truth, and Goodness, about this world and the next.

Part of our response to this mind-reeling act of our loving God in becoming fully human is continually to confess "I believe in ... Jesus Christ, [God's] only Son, our Lord."

For reflection and response

1. Why is it important for Christians to understand and emphasize the full humanity of Jesus?

2. What are the dangers of over-emphasizing Jesus' humanity? How can those dangers be avoided?

3. When facing trials and temptations, how is our faith strengthened by knowing that Jesus Christ was fully human?

Pray and give God thanks for becoming fully human in the person of Jesus Christ. You may wish to pray Isaiah 53:1-12 or to use those verses as a model for your prayer.

Scripture passages for further study

Isaiah 7:14; Matthew 1:18-24; Romans 8:1-5; Galatians 4:4-6; I John 1:1-4.

Additional resources

Wayne Grudem, *Systematic Theology: An Introduction to Biblical Doctrine* (Grand Rapids: Zondervan, 1994).

Daniel L. Migliore, *Faith Seeking Understanding: An Introduction to Christian Theology* (Grand Rapids: Eerdmans, 1991).

J.B. Phillips, *Your God Is Too Small* (New York: Macmillan, 1954).

Bernard Ramm, *An Evangelical Christology: Ecumenic and Historic* (Nashville: Thomas Nelson, 1985).

Parker T. Williamson, *Standing Firm: Reclaiming Christian Faith in Times of Controversy* (Lenoir, NC: PLC Publications, 1996).

9

THE DEITY
OF CHRIST

Suggested Scripture readings
Mark 1:1-11; Mark 9:2-7

Mark 1:1 reads, "The beginning of the gospel about Jesus Christ, the Son of God." Mark's opening declaration, and those of God himself speaking of Jesus in these terms both at Jesus' baptism (Mark 1:11) and transfiguration (Mark 9:7), offer significant support for the historic Christian teaching that Jesus of Nazareth, while fully human, is simultaneously fully God.

Jesus' baptism

Although Scripture and the church's historic confessions are explicit in their affirmations that Jesus Christ was fully human and fully God, one regularly resurgent heresy is that Jesus was "a good man," one who exemplified a superior degree of "God-consciousness," a great moral teacher. But he was not God in human flesh. Those who promote such false teachings often point to Jesus' baptism by John as evidence that Jesus was not divine, arguing that God Incarnate would not submit to being baptized.

But Jesus did not go into the wilderness to be baptized because he believed he was a sinner. Like Moses, Jesus chose not to separate himself from the sins of his people. In submitting to John's baptism, Jesus chose to identify himself with sinful humanity, to acknowledge the justice of God's judgment of sinners, and to affirm that he had become incarnate for the purpose of taking upon himself God's judgment for human sin.

Thus it was as an affirmation of his obedience that, as Jesus was coming up out of the water after being baptized, he saw the heavens open and he heard God's voice from heaven saying, "You are my Son whom I love; with you I am well pleased" (Mark 1:11).

Well pleased with the beloved Son

God's declaration of pleasure with his Son, repeated with a slight variation at Jesus' transfiguration in Mark 9, gives us essential insight into the deity of Christ, and into the relationship between God the Father and God the Son.

In the phrase, "with you I am well pleased," the Greek "I am" is in a grammatical form that implies a past choice for a particular function. We might paraphrase this sentence, "Because you are my beloved Son, *I have chosen you* for the task you are about to undertake." Jesus did not *become* the Son of God, either at his baptism or, as others have argued, at his transfiguration. Rather, at his baptism Jesus already *is* the Son of God whom God loves, as he always has been and forever will be. The opening of the heavens and the heavenly voice do not abruptly alter Jesus' essential nature. Instead, they point to the significance of Jesus obediently fulfilling the task his Father had assigned him.

The phrase "You are my Son whom I love" also yields important insights into Jesus' deity, for the tense and mood of the verb translated "you are" expresses an eternal, essential relationship. To say that the relationship between God the Father and God the Son is eternal is to acknowledge that Jesus was the Son of God before the creation of time, and that Jesus will continue to be God's Son after time has ended.

"The New Testament, in hundreds of explicit verses that call Jesus 'God' and 'Lord' ... affirms again and again the full, absolute deity of Jesus Christ."

— *Wayne Grudem*

Although it is hard for us to grasp, time itself is simply one of God's creations. Time had a definite beginning and will have an equally definite ending. In contrast, Jesus' relationship to God has neither beginning nor end. Jesus always was, now is, and forever will be God's Son.

The "essential" aspect of Jesus' relationship to God the Father has caused considerable confusion and division throughout the history of the church, for it indicates that Jesus Christ and God the Father are "in essence" – that is, in substance, in composition, in the very nature of their uncreated being – one and the same. The essential nature of Jesus Christ was the single most divisive issue for the church's first four hundred years. The longest article of what we now know as the Nicene Creed is devoted largely to Jesus' essential nature. It reads in part:

> Jesus Christ, the only-begotten Son of God: begotten of His Father before all worlds: God of God; Light of Light; Very God of Very God; Begotten, not Made; Being of one substance [*homoousia*] with the Father.

Although some today may find such language redundant, or even outdated, in the fourth century each of these phrases was a battleground, as much an issue for the church as the nature and authority of Scripture is today. (For an explanation of the issues at stake in Nicea and an exploration of the significance of these issues for today's Christians, see Parker T. Williamson's *Standing Firm: Reclaiming Christian Faith in Times of Controversy* [Lenoir, NC: PLC Publications, 1996]).

In the language of classical theology, the issue was nothing less than the deity of Christ. In simpler terms, the question being debated was: "Is Jesus Christ really God?"

The unanimous answer of historic Christian orthodoxy to that question has always been a resounding "Yes!"

The New Testament evidence

The phrase "You are my son" only scratches the surface of the New Testament evidence for the deity of Christ. Alister McGrath asks "Why is it important to insist that Jesus is both God and man?" and answers "For a start, the evidence demands that conclusion." Wayne Grudem highlights one segment of that evidence when he observes:

> The New Testament, in hundreds of explicit verses that call Jesus 'God' and 'Lord' and use a number of other titles of deity to refer to him, and in many passages that attribute actions or words to him that could only be true of God himself, affirms again and again the full, absolute deity of Jesus Christ. 'In him *all the fullness of God* was pleased to dwell' (Col. 1:19).

Bernard Ramm adds:

> Even if the direct appellations of deity to Christ are over-statements, the indirect evidence is not, such as the worship Jesus received, his authority to forgive sins, his preexistence, and his claim to have power in himself to perform miracles.

The clear and consistent testimony of Scripture, of Jesus himself, and of God the Father is that Jesus Christ is fully and completely God. The creeds worked out some implications of that revelation in more detail. That Jesus Christ is fully human and fully divine is a difficult, indeed impossible, reality for finite human minds to fully comprehend. But the doctrine is not unreasonable; its truth is simply beyond the limited capacities of human reason.

Jesus Christ, God's only Son

The third Christian millennium is an age when far too many are all too willing to declare that Jesus Christ is not divine, not the unique Son of God, not "of one substance with the Father." When engaged in such debates we need to recall that 1,600 years ago this same battle was fought, and won, at the Ecumenical Council of Nicea. We also need to remember that 300 years before that it was "For this reason the Jews tried all the harder to kill [Jesus]; not only was he breaking the Sabbath, but he was even calling God his own Father, making himself equal with God" (John 5:18).

There is comfort and assurance in remembering that our voices sound in unison with Scripture, the earliest Christians, and the Reformers each time we confess our faith, "I believe … in Jesus Christ, [God's] only Son."

For reflection and response

1. Why is the deity of Christ periodically challenged?
2. Why is it inadequate to describe Jesus simply as "a good moral teacher?"
3. What evidence is there for the historic Christian belief that Jesus Christ is fully God as well as fully human?
4. If Jesus is not God, what are the implications for Christian faith and life?

Pray and give God thanks that his son Jesus became fully human while remaining fully God. You may wish to pray Rev. 5:9-13 or to use those verses as a model for your prayer.

Scripture passages for further study

Matthew 9:1-6; John 1:1-14; John 5:8-18; John 20:24-28.

Additional resources

Wayne Grudem, *Systematic Theology: An Introduction to Biblical Doctrine* (Grand Rapids: Zondervan, 1994).

Murray J. Harris, *Jesus as God* (Grand Rapids: Baker, 1992).

I. Howard Marshall, *Jesus is the Christ: Studies in the Theology of John* (Grand Rapids: Eerdmans, 1989).

I. Howard Marshall, *The Origins of New Testament Christology*, updated edition (Downers Grove: InterVarsity Press, 1990).

Alister McGrath, *I Believe: Understanding and Applying the Apostles' Creed* (Grand Rapids: Zondervan, 1991).

Bernard Ramm, *An Evangelical Christology: Ecumenic and Historic* (Nashville, Thomas Nelson, 1985).

10

JESUS OUR LORD

Suggested Scripture readings
Philippians 2:5-11; Romans 10:6-10; I Corinthians 8:5-6

At seminary I studied Presbyterian history and theology with Dr. Edward Dowey, who, during a lecture on the Westminster Confession, mentioned almost in passing Philippians 2:11, "every tongue should confess that Jesus Christ is Lord, to the glory of God the Father."

But after quoting that verse, he paused and slowly repeated the words "Jesus Christ is Lord." Then, with an intensity that conveyed his desire to implant this truth into the core of our beings, he proclaimed, "That is *the fundamental confession* of our Christian faith. Jesus Christ is Lord." This esteemed theologian, a scholar of worldwide renown, a man who had devoted himself to mastering the nuances and details of the great Christian creeds and confessions, stood before a group of seminary students and declared with every fiber of his being that the foundational confession of the Christian church is "Jesus Christ is Lord."

In the last two chapters we have sought to understand the implications of Jesus' full humanity and his full deity. In this chapter we will consider what it means for Christians to affirm those words of the Apostles' Creed that declare that Jesus Christ, God's only Son, is "our Lord."

The word "lord" in the New Testament

Kyrios, the Greek word translated "lord," is used in several different ways in the New Testament. It is used as is our English word "sir," as a title of respect, particularly when addressing an older person or person of a higher social class. It was also used to mean a master, one who owned property or slaves. Occasionally *kyrios* referred to political rulers, corresponding to the Latin *dominus*. And it was also used of the gods, those divine beings who have power and rights over humankind.

The most significant New Testament example of this last usage may be traced back to the Old Testament, where the four Hebrew letters YHWH represented the name of God by which God revealed himself to Moses at the burning bush (Ex. 3:14). Over time, the Jews became reluctant to say this name aloud, lest they blaspheme God by the accidental mispronunciation of his name. So it became their custom to substitute *adonai*, the Hebrew word for "lord," whenever they came to YHWH in their reading of the Scriptures. When the Hebrew Scriptures were translated in to Greek, *adonai,* was translated *kyrios*.

I. Howard Marshall observes:

> The New Testament does not often call Jesus God directly, but it certainly takes over the Old Testament use of kyrios to refer to God and reapplies it to Jesus. Passages of Scripture that originally applied to God are reapplied to Jesus, thereby showing a tacit identification of Jesus with the Lord spoken of in the Old Testament." So for the first Christians to confess Jesus Christ as their Lord was not merely to accept his authority over their lives, although it certainly was that, it was also to proclaim that Jesus Christ was fully God.

It is of more than passing interest to note that in the Roman empire the phrase *kyrios kaiser*, "Caesar is Lord," was used to proclaim the deity of the emperor. The first-century Jewish historian Josephus wrote that the Jews

Unless we confess – with both hearts and minds,
with both words and deeds – that Jesus Christ is
our Lord, we will inevitably find ourselves under
the dominion of another ruler.

---

refused to call the Roman Emperor *kyrios* because they reserved that name for God alone. Later, Christians who affirmed that Jesus, not Caesar, was Lord were put to death, preferring to die than to render unto Caesar that which did not rightfully belong to him.

In our own century, when Adolph Hitler came to power and demanded that his government have authority over German churches, a courageous group of Christians met in Barmen and produced one of Christendom's most compelling affirmations of Jesus' lordship, "The Theological Declaration of Barmen," which reads in part:

> Jesus Christ, as he is attested for us in Holy Scripture, is the one Word of God which we have to hear and which we have to trust and obey in life and in death. We reject the false doctrine, as though the Church could and would have to acknowledge as a source of its proclamation, apart from and besides this one Word of God, still other events and powers, figures and truths, as God's revelation (8.11).

Jesus as Lord

Throughout the gospels, those who addressed Jesus as "Lord" recognized him as one who gave commands to be obeyed, not merely advice to be considered. While some have argued that "Lord," in the sense of one who has authority and power, is a title ascribed to Jesus only after his death, Marshall answers, "If Jesus is Lord after his resurrection, it is obvious that he must also have been Lord before it. The early church saw the resurrection as essentially the confirming of a status rather than the conferral of a new status."

The eternal lordship of Jesus Christ is a prominent theme in the writings of Paul, especially in Romans and I Corinthians. Paul tells the Christians in Rome "That if you confess with your mouth 'Jesus is Lord,' and believe in your heart that God raised him from the dead, you will be saved" (Rom. 10:9). And he reminds the Corinthians that "for us there is but one God, the Father, from whom all things came and for whom we live; and there is but one Lord, Jesus Christ, through whom all things came and through whom we live" (I Cor. 8:6).

Neither the general concept of lordship, submitting oneself to the demands of a higher authority, nor the historic Christian understanding of Jesus Christ as our one Lord is very popular today. Instead, much of our culture, and many in our churches, subscribe to a belief in "radical autonomy." Although advanced in various guises, the root of this distinctly anti-Christian doctrine is the prideful assertion that there is no higher law than our own wants and needs, and that therefore we are required to obey no authority outside ourselves.

The fruits of this doctrine are evident in theologies that elevate personal experience over God's self-revelation and in systems of belief that deny the transcendence of God. For when God is reduced to a subset of our inner thoughts and feelings, or when every human being is deemed to be a fully functional god (or goddess), the affirmation "Jesus Christ is Lord" becomes at best an irrelevant anachronism, at worst an intolerable impediment to self-actualization.

That is why the "fundamental confession of our Christian faith" has always been, and must always be, "Jesus Christ is Lord." For unless we confess – with both hearts and minds, with both words and deeds – that Jesus Christ is our Lord, we will inevitably find ourselves under the dominion of another ruler. If we deny the lordship of Christ, it is not a question of whether, but of which lord we will serve.

Jesus our Lord

To be sure, the lordship of Jesus Christ is not unfailingly evident in the lives of his disciples. Despite our best attempts to be Christ's faithful followers, we all stumble from the path of obedience and devotion. As James Boice observes:

> The confession 'Jesus Christ is Lord' on our lips is expectation, at best an acknowledgment of what is only partially true or true in potential. But the day is coming, the day of which [Philippians 2:11] speaks, when the confession will stand as a glorious acknowledgment of what has already taken place. Jesus is Lord. But He will then be Lord completely. There will be no more rivals to His throne.

It is possible to acknowledge Jesus as *a* lord while our attitudes and actions deny that he is *our* Lord. That is why it is essential that we regularly reaffirm "I believe ... in Jesus Christ, [God's] only Son *our* Lord." For each time we proclaim this truth, we remind ourselves that at the very foundation of our faith is our confession of the unalterable, unshakable, nonnegotiable truth "Jesus Christ is Lord."

For reflection and response

1. Why is the confession "Jesus Christ is Lord" foundational to Christian faith and life?

2. Why is it necessary that every Christian submit to Jesus as his or her Lord?

3. Are there areas of your life where you find it difficult to accept Jesus as your Lord?

Pray and give God thanks that Jesus Christ is your Lord and one day he will be recognized as Lord of all. You may wish to pray Psalm 2 or to use that psalm as a model for your prayer.

Scripture passages for further study

Exodus 3:13-15; Matthew 7:21-22; John 8:58-59; Acts 2:14-39; Revelation 19:11-16.

Additional resources

James Montgomery Boice, *Philippians: An Expositional Commentary* (Grand Rapids: Zondervan, 1971).

I. Howard Marshall, "Jesus as Lord" in *Eschatology and the New Testament* (Peabody, Mass: Hendrickson, 1988).

I. Howard Marshall, *The Origins of New Testament Christology,* updated edition (Downers Grove: InterVarsity Press, 1990).

Ben Witherington III, "Lord," in *Dictionary of Jesus and the Gospels* (Downers Grove: InterVarsity Press, 1992).

11

BORN OF THE VIRGIN MARY

Suggested Scripture readings
Luke 1:26-38; Galatians 4:4; Psalm 2:7

"How will this be," Mary asked, "since I am a virgin?"

The angel answered "The Holy Spirit will come upon you, and the power of the Most High will overshadow you."

Among historic Christian doctrines, perhaps only the Resurrection has occasioned more skepticism than the Virgin Birth. It is easy to see how those who deny the existence of God or the possibility of miracles can scoff at the notion of a virgin giving birth. Far more distressing, however, are skeptics in the church, where some now find it fashionable to assert that the Virgin Birth was a literary fiction conceived by the gospel writers to put Jesus on a par with ancient mythological deities. Some even confidently teach that Jesus' conception resulted from Mary's rape by a Roman soldier.

And yet, as they have for centuries, Christians worldwide affirm that Jesus was "conceived by the Holy Ghost, born of the Virgin Mary." What is the biblical evidence for this teaching? Is this doctrine credible in the third Christian millennium? And, if so, what can contemporary Christians learn from it? These are the questions we will address in this chapter.

The biblical evidence

In Roman Catholic theology, the doctrine of the Virgin Birth includes the "threefold virginity of Mary," by which is meant: first, the virginal conception of Jesus without a human father; second, the miraculous birth of Jesus through which Mary physically remained a virgin; and third, the doctrine that Mary remained a virgin after Jesus' birth, never bearing other children or even consummating her marriage with Joseph.

In contrast, the historic Protestant understanding refers only to the virginal conception of Jesus, since only that doctrine has any basis in Scripture. Although some opponents of the doctrine claim that neither Mark, John, nor Paul shows any knowledge of the Virgin Birth, a careful study of Scripture suggests otherwise.

Galatians 4:4 reads, "but when the time had fully come, God sent his Son, *born* of a woman." Here, as in Romans and Philippians, Paul chooses not the Greek word usually used to indicate a mother giving birth to a child, but a word that has as its primary meaning the role of the father in generating a new life. This same word is used in the Greek version of Psalm 2:7, "You are my Son, today *I have begotten you*," or, as it may also be translated, "today I have become your Father."

In Mark 6:3, Jesus is identified as "Mary's son," a noteworthy distinction in an era and society that placed considerable emphasis on the family line of the father. John 8:41 records Jewish religious leaders taunting Jesus, "*We* are not illegitimate children," suggesting that John was quite aware of questions concerning Jesus' paternity. And in his gospel's prologue John declares that those who receive Jesus are "children born not of natural descent, nor of human decision, or of a husband's will, but *born of God*," using the same Greek work Paul chose.

Another important biblical reference is Isaiah 7:14, "The

*"The arguments for rejecting the historicity of the
Virgin Birth seem to me, as I examine them yet
again, not nearly as strong as they are often
assumed to be, and the arguments for accepting it
seem to me weighty."*

　　　　　　　　　　　　　　　　— C.E.B. Cranfield

---

virgin (*almah*) will be with child and will give birth to a son
and will call him Immanuel." *Almah* may be translated either
"virgin" or "young woman." However, in quoting this
prophecy Matthew 1:23 uses *parthenos*, from the Greek
translation of the Old Testament, a word that specifically
means "virgin." While this translation probably would not
suggest a virginal conception to one who did not already
have the idea in mind, Isaiah's prophecy would have provided
a welcome confirmation for those familiar with the details of
Jesus' birth.

To be sure, none of these references is a fully expanded
doctrinal defense of the virginal conception, but they are certainly sufficient to counter the suggestion that only Matthew
and Luke had any knowledge (or invented the story) of the
Virgin Birth.

Contemporary credibility

Although some may claim that Christians living in an age
of scientific reason can no longer believe in a virgin giving
birth, it would, in fact, seem easier to affirm this doctrine in
the modern age, when techniques such as in vitro fertilization
and artificial insemination have become commonplace.

Moreover, as R.C. Sproul observes:

That something cannot be duplicated in a controlled laboratory experiment does not mean that it never happened. No
laboratory experiment can eliminate all possible variables.

... In dealing with the virgin birth there is the possibility of a divine omnipotence variable. ... To say the virgin birth is possible is not to prove its truth, but at least it prevents prima facie rejection on alleged grounds that it is impossible.

Following a careful and convincing refutation of theological and historical objections to the Virgin Birth, C.E.B. Cranfield concludes:

> It is, surely, extremely difficult, on the assumption that the Virgin Birth is not historical, to explain at all convincingly how the early Church came during the first century to affirm it, in spite of the fact that there was no expectation [in rabbinical Judaism] that the Messiah would be virgin-born, in spite of the certainty that such an affirmation would be met by incredulity and ridicule among the Jews, in spite of the Church's own interest in maintaining the Davidic descent of Jesus, and in spite of the obvious danger that among Gentiles the doctrine would be misunderstood along the lines of pagan mythology. The arguments for rejecting the Virgin Birth seem to me, as I examine them yet again, not nearly as strong as they are often assumed to be, and the arguments for accepting it seem to me weighty. I have to declare myself convinced that I can, without violating my intellectual integrity, affirm with the Apostles' Creed, without mental reservations and without shuffling, that Jesus Christ 'was conceived by the Holy Ghost, born of the Virgin Mary.'

Modern lessons

Contemporary Christians can learn at least three lessons from the historic Christian doctrine of the Virgin Birth.

First, the Virgin Birth points to the mystery of the personal union between God and humankind in Jesus Christ. The doctrine ultimately at stake in discussions of the Virgin Birth is the Incarnation. In a biblically based theology, the Virgin Birth is neither the basis of, nor evidence for, the Incarnation. Rather, it is the gracious revelation of a loving God who has brought about, in this singular fashion, a true union of deity and humanity.

Second, to confess that Jesus Christ, God's only Son, was "conceived by the Holy Ghost, born of the Virgin Mary" is to acknowledge that Jesus is truly human; that the Word really did become flesh and dwell among us; that the second person of the Trinity did, at a specific moment in time, become a human being even while remaining fully God; that Jesus Christ paradoxically emptied himself by taking on what we are.

And finally, the Virgin Birth attests the fact that God's redemption of his creation is by grace alone. Humanity, here represented by Mary, does nothing more than accept the salvation that has been offered, and even that acceptance is God's gracious gift. As Cranfield writes, "all our pride and self-reliant initiative set aside, our humanity's part is here simply to be made the receptacle of God's gift, to be enabled to submit, to be the object of God's mercy."

In overreacting to some Roman Catholic practices venerating Mary, many Protestants may be overlooking an unparalleled example of humility and obedience. As Sproul notes:

> Mary was chosen by God to make a total, radical, lifelong commitment. The choice was an act of grace that Mary neither sought nor deserved. ... when the time had come and she was asked to do the impossible, she paused at the sheer wonder of it all, then submitted herself completely. This is love for God and courage of the highest order.

How will this be?

"How will this be?" Mary asked.

Gabriel answered, "... nothing is impossible with God."

Not only is the doctrine of the Virgin Birth readily defensible in the third Christian millennium, it is perhaps more important than ever, for it is a startling, even uncomfortable, reminder of the power and sovereignty of God.

For reflection and response

1. Has the historic Christian affirmation of the Virgin Birth ever troubled or embarrassed you? Does the material in

this chapter address any of your concerns?

2. What do you find especially noteworthy about Mary's response to Gabriel's announcement?

3. How does Mary's trust in God inspire your own trust in him?

4. Why is the doctrine of the Virgin Birth important for today's Christians?

Pray and give God thanks for his ability to do in and through us that which seems to be impossible. You may wish to pray I Samuel 2:1-10 or to use those verses as a model for your prayer.

Scripture passages for further study
Matthew 1:18-25; Philippians 2:5-11.

Additional resources
C.E.B. Cranfield, "Some Reflections on the Subject of the Virgin Birth," *Scottish Journal of Theology* (Vol. 44, No. 2, 1988, pp. 177-189).

Richard Longnecker, "Whose Child is This," *Christianity Today* (Dec. 17, 1990, pp. 25-28).

R.C. Sproul, *Renewing Your Mind: Basic Christian Beliefs You Need to Know*, 3rd ed. (Grand Rapids: Baker, 1998).

12

SUFFERED UNDER PONTIUS PILATE

Suggested Scripture readings:
Psalm 23; Isaiah 52:13-53:12; Mark 14:32-42, 15:16-39

Suffered under Pontius Pilate.

In that short phrase the Creed speaks volumes. Obviously it refers to the physical sufferings Jesus experienced as Pilate ordered his flogging and crucifixion (see Chapter 13). But as real and intense as was Jesus' physical agony, the suffering he endured in his soul was more extreme than any human being can imagine. For while far too many people know what it is to undergo enormous physical pain, no mortal can begin to comprehend what it was for the very Son of God to suffer separation from his Father as punishment for our sins.

What we can, indeed must, understand, is that Jesus' suffering is the source of our redemption. It is also of enormous benefit for our daily Christian life to realize that our Redeemer understands our suffering.

The Suffering Servant

To be sure, Jesus' suffering did not come upon him unexpectedly. In Gethsemane, only hours before his crucifixion, Jesus told his disciples, "My soul is overwhelmed with sorrow to the point of death," then he prayed, "Abba, Father, everything is possible for you. Take this cup from me. Yet not what I will, but what you will" (Mark 14:34, 36). His prayer is eloquent testimony to his full humanity, for human nature cannot ignore the fear of suffering.

Not only did Jesus anticipate the suffering he would soon endure to save us from our sins, but that agony had been prophesied hundreds of years before. "Surely he took up our infirmities and carried our sorrows, yet we considered him stricken by God, smitten by him, and afflicted. But he was pierced for our transgressions, he was crushed for our iniquities; the punishment that brought us peace was upon him, and by his wounds we are healed" (Isa. 53:4-5).

In humble obedience to the will of his heavenly Father, Jesus suffered so that our sins would not separate us from God for all eternity. That suffering led to what was no doubt the most agonizing utterance of any human being, Jesus' cry of dereliction as our sins separated him from God.

The cry of dereliction

Having been beaten, scourged and nailed to a cross; bearing in his own person the penalty for all human sins; and as a result failing – for the first time in eternity – to feel his Father's presence with him, Jesus instinctively expressed his suffering in biblical language, praying the shattering words of Psalm 22:1, "My God, my God, why have you forsaken me?"

The Greek verb translated "forsaken" means to desert one who is in difficult circumstances. It might be paraphrased "to leave in the lurch." It is impossible for us to comprehend fully the depths of meaning in this cry. Yet we can learn from the fact that even in the inferno of his abandonment Jesus expressed his anguished prayer in a cry of affirmation, "My God, my God."

The beginning of sin is to forsake God; the end of sin is to be God-forsaken. In becoming incarnate, in identifying so completely with sinners, Jesus had offered to bear personally

" To show sufferers that they need not despair, the true Savior became the good teacher by himself epitomizing the truth in his own person."

— Augustine

---

the judgment of God on the human rebellion that separated humanity from God. Now on the cross he who had lived a life of perfect obedience experienced the full alienation from God that this judgment required. His cry expresses the horror of separation from God, the unfathomable pain of real abandonment by the Father.

The sinless Son of God, "who was conceived by the Holy Ghost, born of the virgin Mary, suffered under Pontius Pilate" and as a result of that suffering died the sinner's death, experienced the bitterness of utter God-forsakeness. This was the cost of providing "a ransom for many" (Mark 10:45).

In this terrible moment of desolation, Jesus fully identifies himself with fallen humanity, separated from God by sin. That Jesus has experienced such separation from God means that we need never fear to go to him when we feel cut off from God by our sins. For the One who has promised to be our shepherd has already walked "through the valley of the shadow of death."

The valley of the shadow of death

From the cross Jesus used Psalm 22 to voice his prayer. While some of us may have had occasion to pray those extreme words as well, most of us are perhaps more likely to invoke the more familiar words of Psalm 23.

For we all go through periods of life when it seems as if green pastures have been scorched and still waters dried to rock-hard mud. At times we seem to wander endlessly through the shifting shadows in the valley. We may reach places where we cannot remember, or any more even imagine, what a banquet table would look like. There are times in our lives when we wonder if God knows where we are and what we are going through.

Then we think of Jesus. And we remember, Yes, God knows exactly what I am going through. He has been there. And having been where we are, having first cleared the path he is now leading us along, having walked through a valley of the shadow of death more harrowing than we could ever contemplate, Jesus, the pioneer and perfecter of our faith, now offers himself to us as our Good Shepherd. As he told his disciples, "I am the good shepherd. The good shepherd lays down his life for the sheep" (John 10:11).

Scholars debate the precise meaning of the phrase "the valley of the shadow of death." The Hebrew may be understood to mean "very deep shadow," "total darkness," or to convey the threat of death. What is clear is that regardless of the linguistic derivation of this phrase, the valley of the shadow of death is a fearsome place.

Perhaps it is a place where churning water courses through a narrow channel, threatening to sweep away those desperately trying to scramble out of harm's way. Perhaps it is a twisting, winding place where no trail has been blazed, a place where light glimmers overhead for only a few moments every day. Perhaps it is a place so long and so deep that there seems to be no hope of climbing out of its pit.

The valley of the shadow of death is a place, unique to each of us, where all of us have been. Jesus' suffering reminds us that we have never been there alone. God's people are not spared journeys through the valley. But neither are they condemned to live forever in its shadow. For those who say "The Lord is my shepherd" *walk through* the valley of the shadow of death, faithfully trusting that God will lead us into green pastures beside the still waters.

After all, that is what a shepherd does.

Epitomizing the truth

Jesus, the good shepherd, God Incarnate, second person of the Trinity, "did not consider equality with God something to be grasped, but made himself nothing, taking the very nature of a servant, being made in human likeness. And being found in appearance as a man, he humbled himself and became obedient to death – even death on a cross" (Phil. 2:6-8). Because he did, we now enjoy a restored relationship with a God who understands our suffering even better than we do ourselves.

As Augustine wrote:

> To show sufferers that they need not despair, the true Savior became the good teacher by himself epitomizing the truth in his own person. He participated in our suffering in an empathic way, knowing that through human frailty sorrow might steal in upon our hearts amid afflictions, and knowing that we would overcome it if we yield to God's will above our own, mindful that God knows best those whose well-being he superintends.

For reflection and response

1. Why did Jesus suffer the penalty for our sins?
2. How does the suffering of Jesus help us understand and bear our own suffering?
3. What difference does it make in your life to know that your Lord and Savior is fully familiar with the types of suffering you encounter?

Pray and give God thanks for Jesus' faithful willingness to bear in his own body the penalty for our sins. You may wish to pray Job 3:3-26 or to use those verses as a model for your prayer.

Scripture passages for further study

John 18:28-19:16; Hebrews 4:14-16; I Peter 4:12-19.

Additional resources

Diogenes Allen, *The Traces of God in a Frequently Hostile World* (Boston: Cowley Publications, 1981).

Peter Kreeft, *Three Philosophies of Life* (San Francisco: Ignatius Press, 1989).

Thomas C. Oden and Christopher A. Hall, eds., *Mark* (Downers Grove: InterVarsity Press, 1998).

Herbert Schlossberg, *A Fragrance of Oppression: The Church and Its Persecutors* (Wheaton, Ill.: Crossway Books, 1991).

13

CRUCIFIED, DEAD, AND BURIED

Suggested Scripture readings
Mark 15:12-25; Matthew 27:62-66; I Corinthians 15:3-6

Historically the affirmations of the Apostles' Creed that our Lord Jesus Christ "was crucified, dead, and buried" have been interpreted historically. That is, they have been understood by Christians of all traditions as referring to actual events that took place in the life, and specifically at the death, of a historical human being – God's incarnate Son, Jesus.

But beginning in the late 19th century with the so-called "Quest for the Historic Jesus," some critics have insisted that little, if anything, can be known about the details of Jesus' life. Inexorably these quests have led to such questions as whether Jesus lived at all (see G.A. Wells' *Did Jesus Ever Exist?* [Buffalo: Prometheus Press, 1975]), and even whether Jesus Christ is necessary to Christian faith (as exemplified in feminist theologian Rita Nakishima Brock's avowed intent to construct "a christology not centered in Jesus").

The Jesus Seminar, which spent years casting multi-colored ballots in order to determine that Jesus never said most of what the gospels say he said, has undertaken a project intending to do for Jesus' deeds what it did for his words.

Of course, those who consider Jesus of Nazareth a mere literary fiction, or those who admit his existence yet deem his actual words and deeds unknowable and therefore irrelevant, rightly realize that their presuppositions undermine historic Christian teaching and practice. For to deny that Jesus Christ, God's only Son, our Lord, was crucified, dead and buried is to deny the facts that lie at the foundation of our Christian faith and life.

Historical evidence

Despite the objections of variously motivated critics, the historical evidence for what is claimed in the Creed is substantial and significant. All four gospels report Jesus' trial before Pilate, his crucifixion, and his burial. And Paul, apparently quoting a very early Christian statement of faith, reminded the Corinthians, "For what I received I passed on to you as of first importance: that Christ died for our sins according to the Scriptures, that he was buried, that he was raised on the third day according to the Scriptures" (I Cor. 15:3-4).

The mention of Pilate in the Creed highlights the fact that Jesus' suffering and crucifixion took place at a particular moment in history and in full public view of secular authorities and any Roman citizens or subjects who happened to be in Jerusalem while these events were taking place. As a result, in addition to the biblical accounts, there is also testimony from ancient historians. Perhaps the most widely cited of these comes from the *Annals of Tacitus*, a history of the Roman empire covering the period between Augustus' death in 14 A.D. and Nero's death in 68 A.D. Concerning the great fire in Rome during Nero's reign Tacitus writes:

> Nero fastened the guilt and inflicted the most exquisite tortures on a class hated for their abominations, called Christians by the populace. Christus, from whom the name had its origin, suffered the extreme penalty during the

*"Christus, from whom the name had its origin,
suffered the extreme penalty during the reign of
Tiberius at the hands of one of our procurators,
Pontius Pilate."*

— *Tacitus*

reign of Tiberius at the hands of one of our procurators,
Pontius Pilate.

Other extra-biblical evidence of Jesus' life and death is
found in the writings of Suetonius and Josephus. Of course,
such evidence does not "prove" the truth of the biblical
accounts. But it does make far less tenable the claim that the
gospel accounts are nothing more than pious fiction.

Crucified

That death by crucifixion involves almost unimaginable
physical suffering has long been documented. The ancient
Romans considered it so cruel that they mandated other
forms of execution for their own citizens. A medical journal
article reports:

> Adequate exhalation required lifting the body by pushing up
> on the feet and by flexing the elbows. ... However, this
> maneuver would place the entire weight of the body on the
> tarsals and would produce searing pain. Furthermore, flexion
> of the elbows would cause rotation of the wrists about the
> iron nails and cause fiery pain along the damaged median
> nerves. ... each respiratory effort would become agonizing
> and tiring and lead eventually to asphyxia.

Even more extreme than the physical agony that Jesus
endured on the cross was the spiritual suffering. In attempting
to convey this aspect of Jesus' torment Hans Urs von
Balthasar writes:

'the hour and the power of darkness,' in which every kind of spiritual and physical suffering was inflicted upon him by men, and when even the Father abandoned the tormented one as well, is for us an unfathomable night. No meditation on the Stations of the Cross, not even the horrors of human torturings and concentration camps, can give us a picture of it. What it means to bear the burden of the world's guilt, to experience in oneself the inner perversion of a humankind that refuses any sort of service, any sort of respect, to God, and to do so in view of a God who turns away from these abominations – who can conceive of it?

Dead and buried

But it is perhaps the public death and guarded tomb that most trouble those who would deny the history behind the Creed. In his sermon "The End Is Life," Frederick Buechner paints a vivid picture of the Jewish religious leaders who, after Jesus' crucifixion, asked Pilate to "give the order for the tomb to be made secure until the third day. Otherwise, his disciples may come and steal the body and tell the people that he has been raised from the dead. This last deception will be worse than the first" (Matt. 27:64). As Buechner observes:

> beneath the fear that they spoke about to Pilate lay another fear ... the fear that the man whom they had crucified would *really* come alive again as he had promised, that the body that now lay dead in its tomb, disfigured by the mutilation of the Cross, that this body or some new and terrible version of it would start to breathe again, stand up in its grave clothes and move toward them with unspeakable power.

Preparation for the resurrection

An obvious first line of defense against the unnerving reality, and the eternal implications, of Jesus' resurrection is the claim that we cannot be historically certain that Jesus (if he ever lived) was actually crucified, dead, and buried. For if nothing can be known about the time, place, or cause of

Jesus' death or the details of his burial, then his resurrection can be dismissed as pious fiction, a fraud – perpetrated with only the most noble of intentions – but a fraud nonetheless.

However, Paul's defense of the resurrection in I Corinthians 15 (see Chapters 15 and 16) requires a historical Jesus to have been crucified, dead, and buried. And for Paul – as for John, Peter, James, and the rest of the disciples – the resurrection of the same Jesus who was crucified lay at the heart of the Good News that they faithfully and fearlessly proclaimed.

In asserting that our Lord Jesus Christ "was crucified, dead, and buried," the Apostles' Creed affirms the historical nature of the gospel narratives. In so doing it also lays the foundation for its upcoming affirmation of Jesus' resurrection.

For reflection and response

1. What is the significance of confessing that Jesus was crucified, dead, and buried?

2. What thoughts and feelings must have been going through the disciples' hearts and minds during Jesus' crucifixion? Have you ever been a bystander at a scene that seemed utterly hopeless? What was the result of your experience?

3. How is our reaction to Jesus' crucifixion influenced by our knowledge of his resurrection?

Pray and give God thanks for the fact that Jesus was willing to be crucified as punishment for our sins. You may wish to pray Psalm 22 or to use that psalm as a model for your prayer.

Scripture passages for further study

Isaiah 52:13-53:12; Matthew 27:11-61; John 15:13; John 19:1-16.

Additional resources

Colin Brown, "Quest of Historical Jesus," in *Dictionary of Jesus and the Gospels* (Downers Grove: InterVarsity Press, 1992).

Frederick Buechner, "The End Is Life" in *The Magnificent Defeat* (San Francisco: Harper & Row, 1966).

William Edwards, MD, et al., *Journal of the American Medical Association* Vol. 255, (March 21, 1986, pp. 1455-1463).

Gary R. Habermas, *Ancient Evidence for the Life of Jesus: Historical Records of His Death and Resurrection* (Nashville: Thomas Nelson, 1984).

Hans Urs von Balthasar, *Credo: Meditations on the Apostles' Creed* (New York: Crossroad, 1990).

14

HE DESCENDED
INTO HELL

Suggested Scripture readings
John 5:19-29; I Peter 3:17-4:6

The March 1991 *Journal of the Evangelical Theological Society* contains an article by Wayne Grudem titled "He Did Not Descend Into Hell: A Plea for Following Scripture Instead of the Apostles' Creed." It begins:

> It seems to me that a confession of faith should be repeated only if it represents things one genuinely believes to be true. Yet I personally do not believe that Jesus 'descended into hell' after he was 'buried.' ... my purpose is to give reasons why it seems best to consider the troublesome phrase 'he descended into hell' a late intruder into the Apostles' Creed that really never belonged there in the first place and that, on historical and Scriptural grounds, deserves to be removed.

One year later, the same journal published an article by David P. Scaer titled "He Did Descend to Hell: In Defense of the Apostles' Creed." Scaer begins:

> I can respect Wayne Grudem's decision to omit 'he descended into hell' from his recitation of the Apostles' Creed within the congregation, but I sincerely doubt that he will succeed in winning a sufficient number of adherents to

his cause to effect the change. ... there are good Biblical, historical, and theological reasons for retaining the phrase.

For centuries Christians have been questioning the article of the Apostles' Creed that asserts Jesus Christ "descended into hell." Three main questions include: when and why the phrase was added to the Creed; the exact meaning of the phrase; and what Scripture teaches about this topic. In this study we will briefly consider answers that have been offered to each of these concerns.

The addition of the article

The earliest known versions of the Apostles' Creed, which as we saw in Chapter 2 originated in first-century Rome as a profession of faith to be memorized by candidates preparing for baptism, lack the words "he descended into hell."

However, those who would use this ancient omission to justify deleting this phrase from the Creed must also decide how to deal with the fact that the version known to Iranaeus (ca. 200 A.D.) omits the phrases, "was crucified, dead, and buried"; "the third day"; "sitteth at the right hand of God the Father Almighty"; and "the holy catholic church, the communion of saints, the forgiveness of sins, and the resurrection of the body." Meanwhile, Tertullian's version, dated some 20 years later, adds "the third day"; "sitteth at the right hand of God"; and "the resurrection of the body" but still lacks "the communion of saints" and "the forgiveness of sins."

Given our sketchy knowledge of the Creed's development, it seems that any judgment about "he descended into hell" should be based on more than the slender evidence for when it finally became widely accepted.

The meaning of the article

This brings us to our second question, How, exactly, is this phrase understood by those who say it?

Some suggest that the phrase is merely a restatement of

> *"We ought not to omit his descent into hell, a matter of no small moment in bringing about redemption. [For] it contains the useful and not-to-be-despised mystery of a most important matter."*
>
> — *John Calvin*

"crucified, dead, and buried." This, however, is improbable, for in a statement of faith as compact as the Apostles' Creed, such redundancy would be quite unlikely. Even more telling, as a "clarification," "he descended into hell" raises more questions than the phrase it supposedly explains.

The Heidelberg Catechism asks "Why is there added: 'He descended into hell?'" and answers "That in my severest tribulations I may be assured that Christ my Lord has redeemed me from hellish anxieties and torment by the unspeakable anguish, pains, and terrors which he suffered in his soul both on the cross and before" (Q. 44).

Other widely held understandings of the phrase are summarized by Clayton Bell, who writes:

> The Roman Catholic church takes the phrase 'He descended into hell' to mean that after his death, Christ went into Limbus Patrum, where the Old Testament saints were awaiting the revelation and application of his redemption. He preached the gospel to them, and then he brought them out and led them to heaven. The Lutherans regard the descent into Hades as the first stage of the exaltation of Christ. Christ went into the underworld to reveal, to consummate his victory over Satan and the powers of darkness, and to pronounce their sentence of condemnation. Some Lutherans place this triumphal march between the death of Christ and his resurrection; others after the resurrection. The Church of England holds that while Christ's body was in the grave his soul went into paradise, the abode of the souls of the righteous, and there he gave them a fuller exposition of the truth.

John Calvin interprets the phrase metaphorically, as referring to the penal sufferings of Christ on the cross, where he suffered the pangs of hell while he was hanging in our place.

Which interpretation is correct? I am not sure that it behooves us to be dogmatic on any of them, but one thing I am sure of: that God has left us with some degree of doubt on this matter in order to impress upon us that God did much more for us through the death of Jesus Christ than we have begun to realize or any one interpretation can grasp.

The teachings of Scripture

Several New Testament passages are regularly cited as biblical support for the doctrine of Christ's descent into hell. One is Matthew 12:39-40, where Jesus responds to the Pharisees, "A wicked and adulterous generation asks for a miraculous sign! But none will be given it except the sign of the prophet Jonah. For as Jonah was three days and three nights in the belly of a huge fish, so the Son of Man will be three days and three nights in the heart of the earth."

Proponents of the doctrine point to these verses as evidence that Jesus predicted his descent into hell. However, it is rightly noted that in this statement Jesus does not specifically assert that he will descend into hell, only that he will spend three days and nights "in the heart of the earth," and that the equivalence of "hell" and "the heart of the earth" is by no means self-evident.

Other New Testament writings often cited in this context include John 5:19-29, Acts 2:24-27 and Romans 10:6-7.

But the passages most invoked in discussions of whether Jesus Christ descended into hell are I Peter 3:18-19 and 4:6, which teach that Christ "was put to death in the body but made alive by the Spirit, through whom also he went and preached to the spirits in prison" and "the gospel was preached even to those who are now dead."

Questions raised about these verses include: who are "the spirits in prison" and "the dead," what does the word "preached" mean in this context, what does it mean that Jesus preached "through the Spirit," and do these verses even refer to the same event?

Faithful biblical scholars are divided in their interpretations of these passages, some finding explicit scriptural support for Christ's descent into hell, some finding none at all, many believing that the teaching of Scripture on this topic is more suggestive than definitive. Moreover, some who argue for keeping the phrase in the Creed, John Calvin prominent among them, do not believe that either of these passages supports the doctrine of Christ's descent into hell.

A not-to-be-despised mystery

It was, however, Calvin's opinion that when reciting the Apostles' Creed "We ought not to omit his descent into hell, a matter of no small moment in bringing about redemption. [For] in setting forth a summary of doctrine a place must be given to it, as it contains the useful and not-to-be-despised mystery of a most important matter."

Calvin's insight reminds us that as faithful Christians we have at best a limited understanding of the nature, and many of the actions, of God. Yet despite our imperfect comprehension, we faithfully affirm the mystery of a most important matter each time we confess of Jesus Christ that "he descended into hell."

For reflection and response

1. When you recite the Apostles' Creed, do you say aloud the phrase "he descended into hell?" Why or why not?

2. Which interpretation of the phrase "he descended into hell" seems to have the best biblical and historical support?

3. Should the inclusion or omission of this phrase from the Creed be a major stumbling block to Christians? Should it be discussed at all? Why or why not?

Pray and give God thanks that because of Jesus' death and resurrection we need have no fear of hell. You may wish to pray Psalm 16 or to use that psalm as a model for your prayer.

Scripture passages for further study

Matthew 12:39-40, Matthew 16:18; Acts 2:24-27; Romans 10:6-7; Ephesians 4:8-9.

Additional resources

Clayton Bell, *Moorings in a World Adrift: Answers for Christians Who Dare to Ask Why* (San Francisco: HarperSanFrancisco, 1990).

Wayne Grudem, "He Did Not Descend Into Hell: A Plea for Following Scripture Instead of the Apostles' Creed," in *Journal of the Evangelical Theological Society* (Vol. 34, No. 2, March 1991).

David P. Scaer, "He Did Descend to Hell: In Defense of the Apostles' Creed," in *Journal of the Evangelical Theological Society* (Vol. 35 No. 2, March 1992).

15

THE THIRD DAY
HE AROSE (1)

Suggested Scripture readings
John 20:1-20; Acts 2:22-36; I Corinthians 15:1-11

Would it make any difference to your Christian faith if
there were no resurrection? Would your daily life be any different if you believed that Jesus' body never left his tomb and
that remaining in the tomb therefore would be your eternal
fate as well? In short, would your faith and life be altered if
Christ has not been raised?

For the earliest Christians, these were not idle specula-
tions. The apostles recognized Jesus' resurrection and the
future resurrection of all believers as inseparable truths, realities that give content and meaning to Christian faith. The
Apostles' Creed summarized this essential truth in the phrase
"the third day he rose again from the dead."

John and Peter

"The third day" refers to Easter Sunday and to the discov-
ery of the empty tomb, which reminds us that no human
being witnessed Jesus' resurrection. John tells us that the
empty tomb was witnessed, as were Jesus' appearances to his
disciples. But no one saw what transpired in the tomb
between Friday afternoon, when the stone was rolled across

the entrance of the grave, and Sunday morning, when the women found the stone rolled away.

It was the appearances of the risen Jesus, along with the outpouring of the Holy Spirit, that on Pentecost emboldened Peter to proclaim of Jesus, "This man was handed over to you by God's set purpose and foreknowledge; and you, with the help of wicked men, put him to death by nailing him to the cross. But God raised him from the dead, freeing him from the agony of death, because it was impossible for death to keep its hold on him" (Acts 2:23-24).

A reminder

In I Corinthians 15 Paul offers an extended theological discussion of the resurrection. He begins, "Now I would remind you."

The word "remind" shows us that Paul's intent is not to prove Jesus' resurrection, as if the Corinthians had never heard of the idea, or had heard, yet had not believed. Instead, Paul begins by reaffirming their shared belief in Jesus' resurrection, from which he will develop his arguments against the Corinthian belief that there is no resurrection of the body, a belief that can be traced back to two influences, one Jewish, one Greek.

In Paul's day, one school of Jewish thought, exemplified by the Sadducees, denied that there was any life after death. Therefore they rejected both the immortality of the soul and the resurrection of the body. They based their argument on the observation that the Old Testament has very little to say about life after death. Of course, reading the Old Testament in the light of Easter Sunday, we can easily find references and implications that would have been overlooked by those who lived before Christ's resurrection. But even after Jesus' resurrection, which the Corinthians themselves professed to believe, there still were some who clung to the old beliefs of the Sadducees.

Also in the church at Corinth were those influenced by

*"If Christ has not been raised, your faith is futile
and you are still in your sins."*
— *I Corinthians 15:17*

Greek philosophers who denied the resurrection of the body
for other reasons. Most Greeks believed in the immortality of
the soul – that is, they believed each individual soul had
always existed and would always continue to exist. But for
them, the soul's immortality involved the dissolution of the
body. As William Barclay summarizes:

> We can see this best in the Stoic belief. To the Stoic, God
> was fiery spirit, purer than anything on earth. What gave
> men life was that a spark of this divine fire came and dwelt
> in a man's body. When a man died, his body simply dis-
> solved into the elements of which it was made, but the
> divine spark returned to God and was absorbed in the divin-
> ity of which it was a part. For the Greek, immortality lay
> precisely in getting rid of the body. For him the resurrection
> of the body was unthinkable.

It was such Jewish and Greek beliefs that Paul attempted
to combat by reminding the Corinthians of what they, and all
other Christians, professed to believe. And at the heart of
Paul's reminder lies what many believe to be one of the first
Christian creeds, "For what I received I passed on to you as of
first importance: that Christ died for our sins according to the
Scriptures, that he was buried, that he was raised on the third
day according to the scriptures, and that he appeared to Peter,
and then to the Twelve" (I Cor. 15:3-5).

An early creed

Crucial to this early creed is the verb "was raised." The
Greek is in the passive voice, indicating that Jesus did not

raise himself. Rather, it was God the Father who raised Jesus from the dead, thereby vindicating him, proving once and for all that Jesus Christ was his beloved Son, the one whom God had sent into the world to atone for the sins of the world.

Moreover, unlike the verbs "died, buried, and appeared," which all indicate simple past action, the verb "was raised" is in the perfect tense, which in the Greek indicates past action that remains effective in the present. It would not be too much of a stretch to translate this phrase, "Christ was raised and remains raised." Christ's resurrection was not merely an event that occurred at a past moment in time, although it certainly is no less than that. Christ's resurrection is an event which remains in effect now and throughout all eternity.

Although Scripture records several other incidents of people being brought back to life – the widow's son, the 12-year-old girl, Lazarus – all of those individuals eventually died. Christ's resurrection remains unique, for Christ remains living and active in the world today. Moreover, as we will see in Chapter 16, Christ's resurrection is the anticipation, the firstfruits, of that resurrection of the body promised to all who believe in his name.

Appearances

Paul also declares that Jesus "appeared to Peter, and then to the Twelve. After that, he appeared to more than five hundred brothers at the same time, most of whom are still living, though some have fallen asleep. Then he appeared to James, then to all the apostles, and last of all he appeared to me also, as to one abnormally born" (I Cor. 15:5-7).

The verb translated "appeared" throughout this passage is *ophthe*, "to see," from which we get such English words as ophthalmologist. This Greek root is always associated with seeing as sense-perception, that is with physically apprehending a visible phenomenon.

Such language counters claims that what the apostles and

others described as "appearances" of their risen Lord were only hallucinations, mental aberrations triggered by the stress of Jesus' crucifixion. Again, such charges have long been leveled by those with vested interests in denying the reality of the resurrection. And it is unfortunately easy to find contemporary Christian authors advancing one of many variations on this theme. But what Paul clearly indicates is that Jesus Christ – crucified, dead, buried, and risen – physically appeared, not just once or twice to an isolated individual, but repeatedly to individuals and groups, including one appearance where 500 people saw him.

Paul was passing along to the Corinthians the good news that had been given to him. This good news, Paul reminded them, was the unanimous testimony of the earliest believers. As Paul declares in v. 11, "this is what we preach, and this is what you believed."

You have come to believe that Christ died. You have come to believe that Christ was buried. You have come to believe that Christ was raised. You have come to believe that Christ appeared. Those were the truths that Paul believed and taught. Those remain the truths that all Christians are to believe and teach.

For reflection and response

1. What is the difference between the resurrection of Lazarus (John 11:1-45) and the resurrection of Jesus?
2. Why does Paul place such emphasis on the resurrection?
3. What difference would it make to you if Christ were not raised from the dead?

Pray and rejoice in Jesus' resurrection. You may wish to pray Psalm 121 or to use that psalm as a model for your prayer.

Scripture passages for further study

Mark 5:21-23; Luke 24:13-49; John 11:1-45.

Additional resources

Diogenes Allen, *The Path of Perfect Love* (Boston: Cowley Publications, 1992).

William Barclay, *The Letters to the Corinthians* (Philadelphia: Westminster, 1954).

Gordon D. Fee, *The First Epistle to the Corinthians* (Grand Rapids: Eerdmans, 1987).

Norman Geisler, *The Battle for the Resurrection* (Nashville: Thomas Nelson, 1989).

Merrill Tenney, *The Reality of the Resurrection* (New York: Harper & Row, 1963).

16

THE THIRD DAY
HE AROSE (2)

Suggested Scripture readings
Matthew 28:1-20; I Corinthians 15:12-28

As we saw in Chapter 15, Paul cited as a creed that was believed by all Christians, including those in Corinth: "that Christ died for our sins according to the Scriptures, that he was buried, that he was raised on the third day according to the Scriptures, and that he appeared to Peter, and then to the Twelve" (I Cor. 15:3-5). In I Corinthians 15:12-28, apparently answering those who were teaching that there would be no future resurrection of believers, Paul uses both positive and negative arguments to correct Corinthian misbeliefs about the resurrection.

'If there is no resurrection'

First, in vv. 12-19, Paul argues from the negative. "If there is no resurrection of the dead, then not even Christ has been raised." A broadly expanded paraphrase might read:

> For the sake of argument let's assume that there is no resurrection from the dead. Certainly you realize that the repudiation of a concept in general renders any specific instance impossible. Therefore, in denying the possibility of resurrection in general, you've necessarily denied

Christ's resurrection in particular. For if there is no such thing as resurrection, then Christ can't have been raised.

Here Paul helps the Corinthians see the consequences of what they profess to believe. Jesus Christ was fully human. Jesus died on a cross, in full view of many who were still living and able to testify to that historical reality. Now, Paul says, since it is a verifiable fact that Jesus Christ died, and since you say there is no resurrection, whether or not you intend to, you are claiming that Jesus Christ could not possibly have been raised by God from the dead.

Paul continues, "And if Christ has not been raised, our preaching is useless and so is your faith" (I Cor. 15:14).

The word here translated "useless" means "empty, without basis, devoid of content." Paul says in effect, "If you take away Christ's resurrection, you've got nothing left. My proclamation of the gospel, the proclamation of Peter, Apollos, all the apostles, all the eyewitnesses to the resurrected Jesus – all of these are empty, meaningless. Therefore your faith is useless. What you profess to believe and proclaim is meaningless, utterly without content."

Paul follows this line still farther, "More than that, we are then found to be false witnesses about God, for we have testified about God that he raised Christ from the dead. But he did not raise him if in fact the dead are not raised" (I Cor. 15:15).

With relentless logic, Paul forces the Corinthians to realize that in denying the resurrection they are calling God a liar. To suggest another paraphrase Paul tells them:

> If the fact of the resurrection is untrue, then the testimony to that fact is equally untrue. And even worse, we have borne false witness against God by accusing God of doing something he didn't do – raise Jesus from the dead. If Christ hasn't been raised, then we have been proclaiming a lie in God's name, bearing false witness in the name of the One who commanded, 'Thou shalt not bear false witness.'

He continues by exposing still further consequences of the

> *"Christ's resurrection has set in motion a chain of inexorable events that absolutely determines our present and our future."*
>
> *— Gordon Fee*

Corinthian position, "And if Christ has not been raised, your faith is futile; you are still in your sins. Then those also who have fallen asleep in Christ are lost" (I Cor. 15:17-18).

The word translated "futile" means "pointless, to no purpose." It conveys a sense of deception and of offending what ought to be. While that which is vain is worthless because it has no content, that which is futile is worthless because it is deceptive or ineffective.

What makes such faith ineffective is that the Corinthians' denial of their future – that they are destined for resurrection on the basis of Christ's resurrection – is equally a denial of their past, that they have received forgiveness of their sins on the basis of Christ's death and resurrection. As Paul explained to the Romans, Jesus "was delivered over to death *for our sins* and was raised to life *for our justification.* ... For if, when we were God's enemies, we were reconciled to him through the death of his Son, how much more, having been reconciled, shall we be saved through his life" (Rom. 4:25, 5:10).

Paul recognized that both our justification and our sanctification were inextricably bound together with Jesus' resurrection. To deny one was to deny the other. In effect, Paul is telling the Corinthians that without the resurrection, they cease to be believers altogether. As Paul concludes this portion of his argument, "If only for this life we have hope in Christ, we are to be pitied more than all men" (I Cor. 15:19).

We might summarize Paul's negative argument:

By believing in Christ's death and resurrection we have placed our trust in Christ to forgive our sins. But if Christ has not been raised from the dead, we not only do not have present forgiveness, but we have lost our hope for the future as well. And if we have believed in the future when there is no future, then of all human beings we are the most pitiful – not because Christian existence is interested only in the future, but because the loss of the future means the loss of our past and present as well.

The firstfruits

In I Corinthians 15:20-28 Paul uses a positive argument, showing the necessity of Jesus' resurrection and the inevitability of the future resurrection of believers. Saying that raising Christ from the dead is the most fitting solution God could have devised to the human condition, Paul begins, "But Christ has indeed been raised from the dead, the first-fruits of those who have fallen asleep" (I Cor. 15:20).

The term "firstfruits" has rich biblical overtones, referring specifically to the commandment in Leviticus 23 to conse-crate the firstfruits of a harvest to God. Here Paul uses the term as a metaphor for the first of the harvest serving as a kind of guarantee for the full harvest. The firstfruits are thus a present pledge on the part of God, a down payment on the eschatological harvest, the resurrection of all believers. God's pledge is that there will be a full harvest. In calling Christ the firstfruits, Paul assures the Corinthians that the resurrection of believers is absolutely inevitable – it has been guaranteed by God himself.

Paul continues "For since death came through a man, the resurrection of the dead comes also through a man. For as in Adam all die, so in Christ all will be made alive" (I Cor. 15:21-22). By sinning, Adam consciously separated himself from God, thereby from Life itself. Death, the common lot and certain fate of humankind, is the result of our being "in

Adam," that is, of our being born of his race and thereby involved in the sin and death that proceeded from him.

However, those who are now "in Christ," those who have entered the new humanity through grace by means of his death and resurrection, will just as certainly be made alive.

Making a difference

What difference does it make in your Christian faith and life that on the third day Jesus Christ rose again from the dead? Gordon Fee answers:

> The resurrection of Christ has determined our existence for all time and eternity. We do not merely live out our length of days and then have the hope of resurrection as an addendum; rather, as Paul makes plain in this passage, Christ's resurrection has set in motion a chain of inexorable events that absolutely determines our present and our future. Christ is the first fruits of those who are his, who will be raised at his coming. That ought both to reform the way we currently live and to reshape our worship into seasons of unbridled rejoicing.

For reflection and response

1. What are reasons you have heard people give for not believing in Jesus' resurrection? What biblical responses can you give to these objections?

2. In your own words, summarize the two arguments Paul makes in these verses.

3. How does belief, or disbelief, in the resurrection influence the way a person lives?

Pray and give God thanks that Jesus' resurrection is the guarantee of our resurrection. You may wish to pray Job 19:25-27 or to use those verses as a model for your prayer.

Scripture passages for further study

Leviticus 23:1-22; Hebrews 2:9-15; Romans 4:23-5:10.

Additional resources

Diogenes Allen, *The Path of Perfect Love* (Boston: Cowley Publications, 1992).

Gordon D. Fee, *The First Epistle to the Corinthians* (Grand Rapids: Eerdmans, 1987).

Norman Geisler, *The Battle for the Resurrection* (Nashville: Thomas Nelson, 1989).

Merrill Tenney, *The Reality of the Resurrection* (New York: Harper & Row, 1963).

17

HE ASCENDED INTO HEAVEN

Suggested Scripture readings
Luke 24:50-53; Colossians 3:1-4

The pace and the pattern of modern life can be dizzying as
the demands of secular society pull us in many different
directions. When we find ourselves being pulled away from
God, one stabilizing resource can be found in the affirmation
of the Apostles' Creed that Jesus Christ "ascended into
heaven and sitteth at the right hand of God the Father
Almighty." For Christ's ascending into heaven and sitting at
God's right hand are not abstract assessments of academic
theology. Rather, as Luke and Paul both show us, these truths
are timely realities that can help us meet the demands of
modern life.

Ascended into heaven

Luke ends his gospel where it began, in the temple,
thereby reminding us that the worship of God is essential to
the people of God:

> When [Jesus] had led [the disciples] out to the vicinity of
> Bethany, he lifted up his hands and blessed them. While he
> was blessing them, he left them and was taken up into
> heaven. Then they worshiped him, and returned to Jerusalem

with great joy. And they stayed continually at the temple, praising God (Luke 24:50-53).

Even though the disciples had not been expecting this to be the last time they saw their risen Lord, once he took his final leave of them, they returned to Jerusalem "with great joy." No doubt there was an immediate sorrow that Jesus would no longer be physically among them. But the disciples' ultimate reaction to Jesus' departure reminds us that, despite the flux of human life, one abiding characteristic of God's people is "great joy."

Situations change. Individuals come and go. Children are born into a family – you blink and they have left for college. One practical lesson of the doctrine of Christ's ascension is that comings and goings have always played a part in the lives of Christ's followers. Yet even when such transitions are unexpected, they can become opportunities for great joy and for the worship of God.

The disciples seemed to be expecting that Jesus was ready to bring about the kingdom of God in all its fullness. Instead, his ascent into heaven set the stage for the coming of the Holy Spirit, bringing humanity's relationship with God into a new era.

The meaning of the ascension

The theological significance of the ascension seems to have received very little attention in recent Protestant thought. That is an unfortunate oversight, for as John Leith writes:

> The ascension means that the earthly ministry of Jesus has ended ... that the incarnate life of Jesus Christ is taken into the very being of God; that the ministry of Jesus Christ, formerly limited by space and time, is now universal by the power of the Spirit of God; that Jesus Christ is at the right hand of God; that he makes continual intercession for us and has opened for us the way to the presence of God; and that he has been given all authority in heaven and earth.

*"The ascension means ... that the ministry of
Jesus Christ, formerly limited by space and time,
is now universal by the power of the Spirit of
God."*

— John Leith

The ascension marks the end of the revelation of Jesus Christ
and the beginning of the work of the Holy Spirit, making his
presence alive in all the world. ... The doctrine of the ascension intends in the words of ordinary experience and of
space to describe that which is beyond ordinary experience
and is not contained in the space we know ... that a new
epoch in human history has begun with the sending of the
Spirit and the mission of the church.

The mission of the church, the task of sharing the Good
News, has been passed down from the disciples through each
succeeding generation to each of us. Jesus' work on earth is
now ours to do, for Jesus Christ our Lord has ascended into
heaven where he now is sitting "at the right hand of God the
Father Almighty."

At the right hand of God

Paul emphasizes the significance of the ascension when he
tells the Colossians "Since, then, you have been raised with
Christ, set your hearts on things above, where Christ is seated
at the right hand of God. Set your minds on things above, not
on earthly things" (Col. 3:1-2). As Peter T. O'Brien explains
this language:

Paul is not indicating an interest in some cosmic geography ...
[His language] has to do with what is ultimately essential,
transcendent, and belonging to God.

Elsewhere Paul describes this same contrast as between
the realms of the flesh and the Spirit. For example, in Romans

8:5 he writes, "Those who live according to the sinful nature have their minds set on what that nature desires; but those who live in accordance with the Spirit have their minds set on what the Spirit desires."

Certainly Paul is not repudiating "living in the flesh" in the sense of living as a human life on earth. For even though corrupted by sin, the flesh is part of God's good creation. Rather, what Paul rejects is the orientation of life toward the flesh, toward that old order to which the Christian no longer belongs. Having died and been raised with Christ, the Christian's proper orientation is toward the realm of those things that are above.

The fundamental reason for seeking the life of the Spirit, for setting one's mind on the things that are above, is that this is the realm where Christ is. Again Paul's language, like that of the psalm he is quoting, is figurative. Ancient Jews and Gentiles alike commonly regarded the right side as a position symbolic of honor or good fortune. They no more thought of a literal, physical right hand of God than we do. Instead, this messianic interpretation of Psalm 110 emphasizes the present reality of Christ's exaltation by God the Father. The heavenly realm, which Christ's disciples are to seek and set their minds upon, thus centers around the resurrected Christ, who now reigns with God in heaven.

The Greek words translated "seek" and "set your mind" both express not simply an activity of the intellect, but also an act of the will. Both show that Christ's followers must continually strive toward that to which they would not naturally tend, to allow our every thought and word and deed to be directed by the ascended Christ, who now sits at the right hand of God.

Things above

My sister-in-law is a dancer and a dance instructor. After performing outdoors one cloudless day she remarked on how challenging it had been to dance in such conditions, for the absence of clouds made it impossible to use a technique known as "spotting."

Spotting involves fixing your eyes on a particular point above you, then keeping your head still and your eyes fixed on that spot for as long as possible into your turn. At the last moment, you whip your head around then pick up the spot again. This causes only minimal movement of the fluid in your inner ear, which means you have a much better chance of keeping your balance.

But when dancing outside on a cloudless day, the sky leaves you nothing to spot. When I asked how dancers compensated, she told me that experienced dancers can visualize a spot even where there is no physical object. That way they keep from getting dizzy no matter how complex the choreography, no matter how unfavorable the immediate surroundings.

What dancers call "spotting," Paul calls setting your heart and mind on things that are above.

Modern life can be dizzying. But if we set our hearts and minds on things above and not on things of earth, we will be far less likely to be pulled away from God and disoriented by the fads and trends that serially captivate the world in which we live.

And we set our minds on things above each time we confess our faith in Jesus Christ, who ascended into heaven, and sitteth on the right hand of God the Father Almighty.

For reflection and response

1. Why is Christ's ascension important to our Christian faith and life?

2. Have you heard many sermons or Sunday school lessons on the ascension? If not, why do you think this doctrine has not received more attention?

3. What are some specific ways in which you can set your heart and mind on things above?

Pray and give God thanks that Jesus is now at his right hand praying for us. You may wish to pray Psalm 24 or to use that psalm as a model for your prayer.

Scripture passages for further study
Psalm 110; Acts 1:1-11; Romans 8:3-11; Hebrews 12:1-3.

Additional resources
John Leith, *Basic Christian Doctrine* (Louisville: Westminster/John Knox Press, 1993).

Peter T. O'Brien, *Colossians-Philemon* (Dallas: Word, 1982).

18

HE SHALL COME TO JUDGE

Suggested Scripture readings
Matthew 24:36-47; Revelation 20:11-15

"Shall" is one of presbyterianism's favorite terms. Throughout the *Book of Order* (part of the Presbyterian Church constitution), "shall" appears each time a practice or procedure is deemed mandatory. One observer even described a denominational restructuring as an effort to decide "Who may 'shall' whom."

Of course, the force of any human use of "shall" is mitigated by the ability of people to respond, "No, we shall not." Such limitations remind us that saying "shall" with absolute assurance is the prerogative of God alone. That is why we should pay rapt attention to that phrase of the Apostles' Creed that declares of Jesus Christ, "he *shall* come to judge the quick and the dead." For in this article of the Creed we learn of two certain future acts of Jesus Christ: first he shall come, then he shall judge.

The *parousia*

In Matthew 24:36-44, Jesus is addressing his disciples' question, "what will be the sign of your coming and of the end of the age?" He tells them, "No one knows the day or hour, not even the angels in heaven, nor the Son, but only the Father. As it was in the days of Noah, so it will be in the days of the coming of the Son of Man."

The Greek word translated "coming" in the disciples' question and Jesus' answer is *parousia*, which can mean either, "to come," or "to be present with" (see Phil. 2:12). The language of God's "coming" and "being present" also has a rich history in the Old Testament (see Joel 2:1; Psalm 139:7). Most often, however, the New Testament writers use *parousia* as a technical term to describe Jesus' second coming, his glorious return from heaven to earth, when he will establish God's kingdom in all its fullness.

Although Jesus' second coming has been the subject of considerable speculation, not all of it helpful, the doctrine of the *parousia* is important because of its implications for the doctrines of christology (the person and work of Jesus), eschatology (the end times) and salvation. In the words of Larry J. Kreitzer, the *parousia* serves as "the culmination of God's eternal purposes as they are worked out in human affairs and as the time at which the world is judged and believers are granted resurrection existence and are ultimately united with their Lord."

Paul, Peter, James and John all write of Christ's *parousia* in their letters, using this same word in this same sense. And when the disciples ask Jesus about the end of the age, their question to him is, "What will be the sign of *your* coming?"

The signs

Jesus answers: "As it was in the days of Noah, so it will be at the coming of the Son of Man" (Matt. 24:37). In other words, until the very moment of his arrival, the day of Jesus' second coming will be pretty much like any other day. People will be going to work and school, planning and attending meetings, eating and drinking, marrying and giving in marriage. Jesus' emphasis is not on the wickedness of those

"If dying love wakens in us ... an answering love,
turning us from sin, then God's wrath achieves its
end through the victory of his mercy."
— *Austin Farrer*

---

swept away by the flood, but on their unpreparedness. Noah had preached, but the people, utterly self-absorbed, had refused to hear his message. By the time they finally recognized that Noah had been asking them to choose life over death, it was too late.

At Jesus' *parousia*, such unpreparedness will be inexcusable. The Old Testament had accurately predicted Jesus' Advent. The New Testament predicts Jesus' *parousia* and says that the principal sign of his second coming will be our routine involvement in the stuff of daily life. That is why we are called to be ready, to be alert, to live in the constant expectation of Jesus' imminent return. For the Apostles' Creed reminds us not only that Jesus shall come, but that when he does he shall "judge the quick [that is, the living] and the dead."

The coming judgment

The scene described by John in Revelation 20:11-15 is popularly known as "the Great White Throne Judgment." While interpretations of this particular vision (indeed of most of Revelation) vary widely, most commentators agree that this scene describes a future judgment.

In John's earlier visions, God's throne is seen the center of worship, the focus of attention, and the source of indescribable joy. It is also the ultimate and eternal center of all authority. For those who acknowledge this authority and are willing to be guided by it, God's throne is the source of wholeness, meaning, and purpose for our lives.

But one day even those who now reject God's authority will recognize it. A consensus of commentators recognizes that those judged at this throne are those who had rejected Jesus Christ while they were living. John describes these individuals as being judged according to what they have done as recorded in the books. This passage nowhere teaches salvation by works, for none is said to have been saved by what he has done. Rather, the works here described lead not to salvation, but to eternal separation from God.

Mercy experienced as judgment

What will be the sign of Christ's coming and of the end of the age? "As it was in the days of Noah, so it will be in the days of the coming of the Son of Man."

To Noah and his family, the coming of the flood was the fulfillment of God's promise. To those who ignored Noah's warning, the flood meant death. So it will be with the second coming, the *parousia*, of Jesus. To those who have heard and believed his message, his coming will be seen as the fulfillment of his promise. Those who have ignored the gospel will experience this same coming as catastrophe.

God's love and God's wrath, God's mercy and God's judgment are simply two sides of the same coin, a single reality experienced from opposite perspectives. Austin Farrer expressed this truth with compassion and eloquence:

> Light is named by contrast with darkness, health with sickness, sanity with madness. In any one of these oppositions, unless I understand the meaning of both the opposites, I can attach no sense to the name of either. If I am to rejoice at the presence of light I must be able to feel the threat of darkness. ...
>
> The death of Christ has been called the reconciliation of God's wrath and love; but they need no reconciliation, they are one in God, and the perfect unity between them is expressed in Christ's death. (How he hates sin, for he dies to

destroy it; and how he loves sinners, for he dies to rid them of it.) ...

If dying love wakens in us, though slowly, an answering love, turning us from sin, then God's wrath achieves its end through the victory of his mercy. But if not, then in the last resort the tables are turned, and God's mercy takes effect through his wrath. His mercy to his whole creation and his love for its perfection must take effect in the banishment of irreconcilable enemies to an outer darkness having no common boundary with the world of light.

May we be reminded of these certainties each time we confess our faith in Jesus Christ, God's only Son, our Lord, who "*shall* come to judge the quick and the dead."

For reflection and response

1. Why is the doctrine of Christ's second coming important?
2. What does it mean to say that God's mercy "takes effect through his wrath?"
3. Are you comforted or concerned (or both) at the thought of Jesus coming to judge the living and the dead? Why?

Pray and give God thanks that Jesus shall come again. You may wish to pray Psalm 9:1-8 or to use that psalm as a model for your prayer.

Scripture passages for further study

Psalm 75; Psalm 96; Isaiah 55:6-7; Ezekiel 33:10-20; Daniel 7:13-14; Joel 2:1-11; John 3:16-21; I Thessalonians 4:13-18; II Thessalonians 1:5-2:4; Revelation 22:16-21.

Additional resources

Austin Farrer, *Lord I Believe: Suggestions for Turning the Creed into Prayer* (Cambridge, Mass: Cowley Publications, 1989).

Paul Ferguson, "Second Coming of Christ" in *Evangelical Dictionary of Biblical Theology* (Grand Rapids: Baker, 1996).

Larry J. Kreitzer, "*Parousia*" in *Dictionary of the Later New Testament and its Developments* (Downers Grove: Inter-Varsity Press, 1997).

Eugene Peterson, *Reversed Thunder: The Revelation of Saint John and the Praying Imagination* (San Francisco: Harper & Row, 1988).

R.C. Sproul, *The Last Days According to Jesus* (Grand Rapids: Baker, 1998).

19

THE PERSON OF THE HOLY SPIRIT

Suggested Scripture readings
John 14:15-27; Romans 8:1-27

I believe in the Holy Ghost.

Those simple words are all that the Apostles' Creed has to say about the Holy Spirit, less accurately rendered by earlier translators "the Holy Ghost." While God the Father is described as "Almighty," and "maker of heaven and earth," and while the longest portion of the Creed is devoted to explaining who God the Son is and what he did, on the doctrine of God the Holy Spirit, the Creed says nothing more than "I believe."

The doctrine of the Holy Spirit

This seeming inequity is more readily understood as we look back to the origin of the Apostles' Creed in first-century Rome and remember that for the first Christians the fundamental confession of faith, the assertion that so utterly distinguished them from the Jews and pagan religions, was "Jesus Christ is Lord" (Phil. 2:11). All other Christian beliefs and practices, including those concerning the Holy Spirit, flowed from this initial affirmation. So we should not be surprised that this early baptismal creed focused so heavily on Jesus Christ.

Still, the doctrine of the Holy Spirit was neither unknown nor considered unimportant by these earliest Christians. The Holy Spirit is referred to in both the Old and New Testaments. Both the Hebrew (*ruach*) and Greek (*pneuma*) words most often translated "Spirit" throughout Scripture come from roots meaning "wind, breath, spirit." That richness of meaning adds to our understanding of verses such as John 3:8, "The wind blows wherever it pleases. You hear its sound, but you cannot tell where it comes from or where it is going. So it is with everyone born of the Spirit."

Paul offered one of the most important early descriptions of the person and work of the Holy Spirit in Romans 8. Another significant New Testament discussion of the Holy Spirit occurs in Jesus' Farewell Discourse to his disciples, which begins in John 14 and where Jesus tells his disciples: "And I will ask the Father, and he will give you another Counselor to be with you forever" (v. 16).

The word translated "Counselor," here and again in v. 26, is *paraclete*. And in v. 26, Jesus specifically identifies the *paraclete* as "the Holy Spirit." But whether we confess, "I believe in the Holy Ghost," "I believe in the Holy Spirit," or "I believe in the *paraclete*," many Christians are unfortunately unclear about what theologians call the person and the work of the Holy Spirit, more simply, about who the Holy Spirit is and what the Holy Spirit does. Chapter 20 will explore what the Holy Spirit does. Here we will consider who the Holy Spirit is, first by looking at the name *paraclete*.

The paraclete

This Greek *paraclete* combines the verb *kaleo*, "to call," with the preposition *para*, meaning "with, by, beside." Thus a *paraclete* is "someone called alongside." In secular Greek the word was primarily used in the sense of a legal advocate, what we might call a defense attorney. But this is not the only way the term was used. Of the numerous possible English

*"The Spirit is not just something divine or some-
thing akin to God emanating from him ... in giving
us his Holy Spirit God gives us nothing less than
himself."*

— *Thomas F. Torrance*

---

translations for *paraclete*, D.A. Carson writes:

> NIV's 'Counselor' is not wrong, so long as 'legal counselor'
> is understood, not 'camp counselor' or 'marriage counselor' –
> and even so, the Paraclete's ministry extends beyond the legal
> sphere. The same limitation afflicts [the NRSV's] 'Advocate.'
> [The KJV's] 'Comforter' was not bad in Elizabethan English,
> when the verb 'to comfort' meant 'to strengthen, give succor
> to, to encourage, to aid' (from the Latin *confortare*, 'to
> strengthen'). In today's ears, 'Comforter' sounds either like a
> quilt or like a do-gooder at a wake, and for most speakers of
> English should be abandoned. 'Helper' (GNB) is not bad, but
> has overtones of being subordinate or inferior, overtones
> clearly absent from John 14-16.

Carson himself prefers simply to use "Paraclete," which
lacks the potential drawbacks of any single English translation. This same choice is made by Raymond Brown, who, at
the end of a very thorough study of the term, concludes:

> By way of summary we find that no one translation of *para-
> clete* captures the complexity of the functions that [the Holy
> Spirit] has. The *paraclete* is a *witness* in defense of Jesus
> and a *spokesman* for him in the context of his trial by his
> enemies; the *paraclete* is a *consoler* of the disciples for he
> takes Jesus' place among them; the *paraclete* is a teacher
> and guide of the disciples and thus their *helper*. In rendering
> the Greek word into Latin for the Vulgate, Jerome had a
> choice among such Old Latin renderings as *advocatus* and
> *consolator* and the custom of simply transliterating the term

as *paracletus*. In the Gospel he took the latter expedient. We would probably be wise also in modern times to settle for *paraclete*, a near-transliteration that preserves the uniqueness of the title and does not emphasize one of the functions to the detriment of the others.

The third person of the Trinity

Essential to a biblical understanding of the Holy Spirit is recognizing the Spirit as a person, the third person of the Trinity. As Thomas Torrance writes:

> The Spirit is not just something divine or something akin to God emanating from him, not some sort of action at a distance or some kind of gift detachable from himself, for in the Holy Spirit God acts directly upon us himself, and in giving us his Holy Spirit God gives us nothing less than himself. Since God is Spirit, the Giver of the Spirit and the Gift of the Spirit are identical.

As further biblical evidence of the personhood of the Holy Spirit, Torrance observes that the Hebrew word for spirit, *ruach*, unlike *pneuma* in classical Greek thought, "carried an active and concrete sense, so that in linking 'holy' and 'spirit' together, the Old Testament clearly intended the mighty living God, the presence of whose Spirit is to be understood as at once intensely personal reality and dynamic event."

God active in the world

Approaching the question, "Who is the Holy Spirit?" from a slightly different perspective John Leith writes:

> The human spirit is the power by which a person makes himself or herself present and known, so the Holy Spirit is that power by which God makes himself present and known to human beings. The Holy Spirit is God active in the world in the power of the divine personhood.
>
> The word 'spirit' is confusing in ordinary speech, for it sometimes stands in contrast to the material. The spiritual is

popularly thought to be the ethereal over against flesh and blood, which are material. In the New Testament the opposite of spirit is not the material but the impersonal. The spiritual is the personal, and the spirit is the person. Some difficulties in theology are resolved if we remember that the spirit is closely related to what we call the person, and spirituality is closely related to the personal. Each stands in contrast to the impersonal, not primarily in contrast to the material.

The word 'spirit' encounters a second difficulty in common speech: it has no content. There are many spirits loose in the world, and some of them are quite evil. Hence it is crucially important for the Holy Spirit to be defined. For Christians the Holy Spirit is defined by Jesus Christ. Jesus Christ is the concrete revelation of God in human history, and it is through Jesus Christ that we know the Father and that we know the Holy Spirit.

I believe in the Holy Ghost

Who is the Holy Ghost, the Holy Spirit? The Holy Spirit is the third person of the Trinity, our Counselor and Advocate, our Comforter and Helper. The Holy Spirit is a witness to the ministry of Jesus, our teacher and guide. This is whom we confess when we say "I believe in the Holy Ghost."

For reflection and response

1. Does it help you to think of the Holy Spirit as wind or breath? Why or why not?

2. What are the strengths and weaknesses of the various translations of the word "paraclete?" Which do you prefer? Why?

3. Why is it important to understand that the Holy Spirit is a person, not an impersonal force?

Pray and give God thanks for the personal presence of the Holy Spirit. You may wish to pray Psalm 51:10-13 or to use those verses as a model for your prayer.

Scripture passages for further study

Genesis 1:1-3; John 3:5-8; Acts 2:1-21.

Additional resources

Raymond Brown, *The Gospel According to John*, vol. 2 (Garden City: Doubleday, 1970).

D.A. Carson, *The Gospel According to John* (Grand Rapids: Eerdmans, 1991).

John Leith, *Basic Christian Doctrine* (Louisville: Westminster/John Knox Press, 1993).

Zeb Bradford Long and Douglas McMurry, *Receiving the Power: Preparing the Way for the Holy Spirit* (Grand Rapids: Chosen, 1996).

Thomas F. Torrance, *The Trinitarian Faith* (Edinburgh: T&T Clark, 1988).

20

THE WORK OF THE
HOLY SPIRIT

Suggested Scripture readings
John 14:15-27; Romans 8:1-27

In Chapter 19 we affirmed that the Holy Spirit is a person, the third person of the Trinity, our Counselor and Advocate, our Comforter and Helper, a witness to the ministry of Jesus, our teacher and guide. Here we will explore the doctrine of the work of the Holy Spirit, what it is that the Holy Spirit does.

In his Farewell Discourse to his disciples in John 14 Jesus reveals two closely related aspects of the Spirit's work. First, the Holy Spirit communicates truth to the world, second the Spirit reminds and teaches Christ's disciples.

'The Spirit of truth'

Jesus calls the Holy Spirit "the Spirit of truth." Earlier in John 14, Jesus had referred to himself as "the way and the truth and the life." Since God the Father, God the Son, and God the Holy Spirit are One, that means it is accurate to say that the Holy Spirit is truth. However, the Greek grammar here emphasizes not identity, but function. In other words, what Jesus is trying to teach his disciples at this moment is not that the Holy Spirit is truth but that the Holy Spirit communicates truth.

There are countless other spirits loose in the world today. But only God's Holy Spirit, only the *paraclete*, communicates truth to the world. That reality becomes obvious as we look at the results of just a few of these other spirits now active around us. Consider the effects of the spirit of Tribalism in places like Sudan and what once was Yugoslavia. Look at the impact of the spirit of Materialism on our own society. And every few years we are reminded of the dangers of seemingly spirit-filled individuals who draw the misguided, the naïve, and the woefully uninformed to places like Jonestown or Waco.

Compare the fate of those following these spirits of the age with the lives of those who worship the Spirit of Truth. In place of bondage to demagogues or material possessions, those who faithfully respond to the teachings of the Spirit of Truth come to understand, and more important, to exemplify, Jesus' words, "If you hold to my teaching, you are really my disciples. Then you will know the truth, and the truth will set you free" (John 8:31-32). The freedom that comes from loving God, from obeying his commands, and from holding to the teachings of Jesus, is evidence of the Holy Spirit at work in human lives.

This leads to the Jesus' second teaching about the Holy Spirit's work, "the Counselor, the Holy Spirit, whom the Father will send in my name, will teach you all things and will remind you of everything I have said to you" (John 14:26).

Teaching the disciples

It is largely through continual teaching and constant reminding that the Holy Spirit continues to communicate the truth about God the Father and God the Son to Jesus' followers.

For the first disciples, much of the Spirit's work was reminding them of what Jesus had said while he was with them. Remember, as Jesus shared a final meal with them and

"The Holy Spirit is the presence and the power of
God that awakens the human heart and makes
Christian believers alive to the presence of God."
                                    — John Leith

spoke with them one final time on Maundy Thursday evening, the disciples had no idea what was about to transpire. And despite having been told on several occasions, they were absolutely unprepared for what took place on Easter Sunday. It was the work of the Holy Spirit to remind the disciples of what Jesus said and to teach them what he meant.

What the Spirit does in the lives of third millennium Christians is very similar. Consider, for example, reading a passage of Scripture you have read dozens, perhaps hundreds of times, and suddenly hearing something in those words that you had never heard before, something that speaks immediately to a situation you are experiencing. That is the work of the Holy Spirit in your life. Think back to a time when a verse of Scripture came to mind and helped you give wise counsel to a friend, or gave you the strength to continue the struggle. That is what the Holy Spirit does.

Guidance and power

In addition to teaching and reminding us, the Holy Spirit also gives us the guidance and the power to live in a way that conforms to God's will. As Paul wrote, "if you live according to the sinful nature, you will die; but if by the Spirit you put to death the misdeeds of the body, you will live, because those who are led by the Spirit of God are sons of God" (Rom. 8:13-14). Later he adds, "the Spirit helps us in our weakness" (Rom. 8:26).

As Thomas Oden writes:

There is nothing too subtle or dense for the Spirit to penetrate or too sinful for the Spirit to cleanse or too weary for the Spirit to breathe life into again. The Spirit strives with us, prays for us, groans with us.

The Holy Spirit's work in leading us to conform with God's will is often called "sanctification," from a root meaning "holy, set apart." Paul told the Thessalonians "It is God's will that you should be sanctified" (I Thess. 4:3). Sanctification involves not only our spirits, but our bodies and our minds, "offer your bodies as living sacrifices, holy and pleasing to God ... be transformed by the renewing of your mind" (Rom. 12:1-2).

A ministry of peace

What is the result of the Holy Spirit's teaching, empowering, and sanctifying work? Jesus concludes that portion of his Farewell Discourse which deals with the Holy Spirit by telling the disciples, "Peace I leave with you; my peace I give you. I do not give to you as the world gives. Do not let your hearts be troubled and do not be afraid."

When Jesus speaks of "peace" he is speaking of *shalom*, of the ultimate fulfillment of God's messianic kingdom. The word is particularly appropriate in this context, for in ancient as well as modern Hebrew, *shalom* is used to say both "hello" and "good-bye." Jesus was preparing to take earthly leave of his disciples. He was, in a way they could not fully comprehend, telling them "good-bye."

And yet, he was equally welcoming them to a new experience of his presence with the promised coming of the Holy Spirit. Earlier Jesus had told his disciples that he would send them another *paraclete*. Jesus himself had been a counselor and helper, advocate and friend while he was with his disciples. But his absence soon would bring the presence of the Holy Spirit. And the Holy Spirit, then as now, brings peace to the hearts and the minds of the people of God.

A wonderful description of this peace, God's *shalom*, is offered by William Manson:

> The disciples are indeed to have 'peace,' not the world's peace but Christ's. The world gives only to take away. Its peace comes by escape from things rather than by power to endure and overcome them. Its offer does not cover our deepest needs, nor does it compose the strife within. The emperor, as Epictetus observes, can give the world peace from war, but not 'from passion, from grief, from envy.' Christ's peace covers these. He has wrestled with, and overcome, not only the anguish of the present hour, but the spiritual power of the world. He has done something which makes peace in the inward sense possible for believers. Now he bequeaths this peace. His disciples must take it as his last legacy and gift.

This legacy of peace, God's *shalom*, is manifested in our lives by who the Holy Spirit is and by what the Holy Spirit does. As John Leith notes:

> The Holy Spirit is God's personal and powerful presence in the world, who calls forth faith and unites human beings with what God has done for them in Jesus Christ. It is by the power of the Holy Spirit that salvation becomes a reality in human life and in human society. ... The Holy Spirit is the presence and the power of God that awakens the human heart and makes Christian believers alive to the presence of God.

Each time we confess, "I believe in the Holy Ghost" we affirm our faith in the *paraclete*, the Advocate, Counselor, Comforter, Helper, God's personal and powerful presence in the world, the Spirit of Truth, who sets us free by teaching and reminding us of all Christ said and did.

For reflection and response

1. How is the ministry of the Holy Spirit connected to Jesus' ministry?

2. In what ways have you sensed the Holy Spirit at work in your life?

3. What is the difference between the world's peace and Christ's peace?

Pray and give God thanks for the personal presence of the Holy Spirit. You may wish to pray Psalm 104:24-35 or to use those verses as a model for your prayer.

Scripture passages for further study

John 8:27-32; Romans 12:1-21; Galatians 5:16-26; II Timothy 3:14-17.

Additional resources

Raymond Brown, *The Gospel According to John,* vol. 2 (Garden City: Doubleday, 1970).

D.A. Carson, *The Gospel According to John* (Grand Rapids: Eerdmans, 1991).

John Leith, *Basic Christian Doctrine* (Louisville: Westminster/John Knox Press, 1993).

William Manson, *The Incarnate Glory* (London: James Clarke, 1923).

Thomas C. Oden, *Life in the Spirit: Systematic Theology: vol. 3,* (San Francisco: HarperCollins, 1994).

21

THE HOLY
CATHOLIC CHURCH

Suggested Scripture readings
Matthew 16:13-18; Acts 2:37-47

"That the church is an article of faith is made clear by its inclusion in the creed: 'I believe in the holy catholic church,'" writes Thomas Oden.

As by faith we seek to understand what we confess with the phrase, "I believe in the holy catholic church" we will briefly consider each of the last three words in that phrase.

The *ekklesia*

Our modern English word "church" comes from the German *kirche*, which derives from the Greek *kyriakon*, meaning "belonging to the Lord." In the New Testament the word translated "church" is *ekklesia*, which combines the prefix *ek*, meaning "out" or "from" with the verb *kaleo* "to call." The church is thus comprised of "those who are called out." In the Greek version of the Old Testament *ekklesia* was used to translate the Hebrew *qahal*, meaning "congregation, assembly."

Of the 116 NT uses of *ekklesia*, only two are in the gospels, Matthew 16:18 and 18:17. In the first of these, just after Simon Peter confesses, "You are the Christ, the Son of the living God," Jesus declares "on this rock [that is, on this confession] I will build my church, and the gates of Hades will not overcome it." Of this verse Oden writes:

> The personal phrase 'my church' indicates that Jesus ... deliberately intended to form a continuing community of prayer, preaching, and discipline. He called and trained his disciples, and promised the coming of the Holy Spirit to guide them after his ascension. ...

> 'My church,' in Jesus' personal usage, is an indestructible communion of persons who are being upbuilt by their union with him, a communion of which Peter and the apostolic company were the first guardians, to whom were given the task of proclamation of the Word, celebration of the sacraments, and the disciplining of the faithful for eternal accountability.

The church, those who have been called out by Jesus for his service, thus is not a voluntary society, a social service organization, or a political action committee. It is by definition those called forth by the Son to be discipled by the Spirit for the purpose of living lives that bring glory and honor to the Father. That is certainly the picture of the church painted in Acts 2, when, after the day of Pentecost, the three thousand souls who had been added to the church "devoted themselves to the apostles' teaching and to the fellowship, to the breaking of bread and to prayer" (Acts 2:42).

The holy church

The adjective "holy" reinforces the truth that the church consists of those called out by God, for to be holy is to be set apart by God for his service. The church is holy not because of the individual merit of each of its members. Rather, as Ted Dorman writes, "The Church is 'holy' in that it derives its life and sustenance from the Holy Spirit. In everyday experience, the visible Church should give outward evidence of the fruit of the Spirit in its midst through holy living (Gal. 5:22-23).

*"To believe in the church is to live out of the
conviction that grace abides in her, teaches and
governs her common life, and flows from God to
all the faithful."*

— *Thomas Oden*

The mark of holiness does not refer to the actual moral righteousness of its members, however, but to the source of whatever righteousness they exhibit: the Spirit of Christ."

This is a crucial distinction, for it is a grave mistake to join
a local congregation expecting to find there a collection of
sanctified saints. Indeed, as Eugene Peterson notes:

> In no area is disappointment and disaffection in the spiritual
> life as frequent as in the experience (or inexperience!) of
> community. We enter a church looking for God and to our
> dismay find ourselves surrounded by a bunch of fractious
> gossips. ... The most common contemporary North Ameri-
> can response to this is to try to improve the image of
> 'church' by public relations and professional staging. When
> it's successful, which it often is, the results are hard to distin-
> guish in both content and spirit from the world of sales and
> soap operas.

As its history clearly shows, the church has often strug-
gled to understand its holiness. In the fourth century, in the
aftermath of the intense persecution by the Roman emperor
Diocletian, many Christians argued that those who had
denied their faith in the midst of the persecution should not
be readmitted to the church. Against this position, known as
Donatism, Augustine stressed that the Church should not turn
away those who fall away from faith and then return, "provided they exhibit sincere repentance."

Similar debates have raged time and again. As Christianity
enters its third millennium, much of the division between

denominations may be explained in terms of how the holiness of the church is to be understood. Such divisions will not be overcome by further emphasizing that which divides us. Instead, the church will recover its unity only to the extent that it reclaims its identity as a holy people, called out by Jesus Christ and empowered by the Holy Spirit to bear witness to the saving love of God.

The catholic church

The Apostles' Creed also confesses that the church is "catholic," which simply means "universal." The universality of the church is mandated by Jesus in the Great Commission, "Therefore go and make disciples of *all nations*, baptizing them in the name of the Father and of the Son and of the Holy Spirit" (Matt. 28:19). Paul explains, "There is neither Jew nor Greek, slave nor free, male nor female, for you are all one in Christ Jesus" (Gal. 3:28). And the classic theological definition of catholicity was offered in the fifth century by Vincent of Lerins, who defined the catholic, i.e. universal, nature of Christian belief as "that faith which has been believed everywhere, always, by all."

Since the Apostles' Creed originated a thousand years before what we now call the Roman Catholic Church, English translations of the Apostles' Creed should (but do not always) print this word with a lower case "c." Indeed, some contemporary English translations of the Creed, in order to avoid this potential confusion, use the phrase "the holy *universal* church."

While that phrase may not roll comfortably off the tongue, it does convey the sense of the Creed, and it accurately expresses the reality depicted in Acts 2 – that all believers are one in Christ, and that therefore there is only one church, a church that includes all Christians, everywhere, throughout all time and eternity.

The congregation of saints

John Calvin wrote, "Wherever we see the Word of God purely preached and heard, and the sacraments administered according to Christ's institution, there, it is not to be doubted, a church of God exists" (*Institutes* 4.1.9). The Lutheran Augsburg Confession similarly describes the church as "the congregation of saints in which the gospel is rightly taught and the Sacraments rightly administered" (Article 7).

We would do well to keep in mind such faithful understandings. As it begins its third millennium, the church as an institutional structure is undergoing a dramatic transition. Old organizational constructs are passing away, and it is not yet clear what new forms will take their place. In such unsettling times it is especially important that Christians not lose sight of the fact that the holy catholic church has been called into being, and will be sustained, by Almighty God. Again quoting Thomas Oden:

> When the faithful confess, 'I believe in the holy catholic church,' the intent is not to displace faith in God with faith in the church. It means that they have faith that there indeed is one holy, apostolic, universal church that has its life in God. To believe in the church is to live out of the conviction that grace abides in her, teaches and governs her common life, and flows from God to all the faithful.

May God grant us the grace and strength, the faith and courage, daily to put into practice all that we affirm each time we confess "I believe in the holy catholic church."

For reflection and response

1. In your own words, describe the nature and function of the church.

2. Is church membership optional for Christians? Why or why not?

3. What do we add to our understanding of the church when we confess that it is "holy" and "catholic?"

Pray and give God thanks for creating and sustaining the holy catholic church. You may wish to pray Psalm 111 or to use that psalm as a model for your prayer.

Scripture passages for further study

Nehemiah 8:1-12; Isaiah 56:4-8; Matthew 28:16-20; Acts 11:1-26; Galatians 5:16-26; Revelation 7:9-10.

Additional resources

Ted M. Dorman, *A Faith for All Seasons* (Nashville: Broadman & Holman, 1995).

Thomas C. Oden, *Life in the Spirit: Systematic Theology: vol. 3* (San Francisco: HarperCollins, 1994).

Eugene H. Peterson, *Leap Over a Wall: Earthy Spirituality for Everyday Christians* (San Francisco: HarperSanFrancisco, 1997).

Miroslav Volf, *After Our Likeness: The Church as the Image of the Trinity* (Grand Rapids: Eerdmans, 1998).

22

THE COMMUNION
OF SAINTS

Suggested Scripture readings
Acts 2:37-47; I John 1:1-4

What do we mean when we confess "I believe in the communion of saints?"

The word "communion" indicates our "common union" with one another as the body of Christ. Calling Christians "saints" is simply another way of saying that we are holy by virtue of our having been called by God into God's service.

We learn more of what this confession means by looking at the closing verses of Acts 2, which describe the days immediately following Pentecost, when the believers "devoted themselves to the apostles' teaching and to the fellowship, to the breaking of bread and to prayer" (Acts 2:42).

The verb translated "devoted themselves" comes from a root meaning "to stay by, to persist at, to remain with." When used of people it has the sense of "loyalty." When used of an object it conveys, "to occupy oneself diligently with, to pay persistent attention to, to hold fast to, continually to be in." In other words, the earliest converts to Christianity did not try to sustain the pure emotion of the Pentecost experience. They did not seek to generate repeated emotional high points as the basis of their common life together. They did not divide into focus groups or subcommittees in an attempt to discern the will of the majority at the moment.

Instead, guided by the Holy Spirit and led by the apostles, the earliest communion of saints paid persistent attention to the apostle's teaching, fellowship, the breaking of bread, and prayer.

The apostles' teaching

These first-century Christians devoted themselves first to "the apostles' teaching." What a privilege and joy it must have been to sit at the feet of those who had spent three years traveling with Jesus. Picture yourself listening to Peter tell about his confession at Caesarea Philippi, "You are the Christ." Imagine your reaction to John, the beloved disciple, as he handed down Jesus' teachings.

While the apostles are not physically present with us, we do have their teachings as recorded in Scripture. We have the gospels: Matthew and John each writing down what he had seen and heard and lived; Mark, according to tradition, putting into writing what Peter preached; Luke the careful historian and traveling companion of Paul authoring a two-volume work, his gospel and the book of Acts.

We also have letters. Many were written by Paul, who did not share the experiences of the 11 who had lived with Jesus, but whose unique encounter with the risen Christ on the Damascus road led to his designation as an apostle. Peter and John also wrote letters. And John, in what is now the last book of the Bible, recorded the Revelation, the Apocalypse, a series of glorious visions shared with him by Jesus.

Are we as devoted as our first-century forbears in the faith to the teachings of the apostles? Do we occupy ourselves diligently with, pay persistent attention to, hold fast to, continually spend time in the Word of God written? If Christians do not continually study and reflect upon the Bible and its lessons

> *"The church is not to drift from one momentary emotional outburst to the next, to resuscitate Pentecost on a weekly basis; rather the church moves immediately to the task of teaching, keeping itself straight about what it is and what it is to be about."*
>
> — *William Willimon*

for our lives, is it any wonder that the church finds itself in disarray? As William Willimon comments:

[The book of] Acts itself was part of the ongoing attempt of the church to reflect upon the implications and applications of the gospel within the church so that the church might continue to be faithful to its calling. The church is not to drift from one momentary emotional outburst to the next, to resuscitate Pentecost on a weekly basis; rather the church moves immediately to the task of teaching, keeping itself straight about what it is and what it is to be about.

Fellowship

Not only did the church devote itself to the apostles' teachings, it was also diligent about fellowship. The Greek word for "fellowship" is *koinonia*, derived from a root meaning "common." It implies participating or sharing with someone or in something. In the New Testament *koinonia* frequently conveys the sense of sharing in a nature that has been received or that is to be attained.

As John writes, "We proclaim to you what we have seen and heard, so that you also may have fellowship [*koinonia*] with us. And our fellowship is with the Father and with his Son, Jesus Christ" (I John 1:3). For Paul, those who share in the Lord's Supper are Christ's companions, they are in fellowship, *koinonia*, with Christ's body and his blood. Such fellowship with Christ necessarily leads to communion with other Christians.

Luke describes the earliest Christians as being absolutely devoted to this *koinonia*. They knew such fellowship wasn't of their own creation but the result of their common union with Jesus Christ. Yet they remained loyal to their *koinonia* with one another. Here we learn a valuable lesson for the contemporary church, the present day communion of the saints: No human program or policy ever creates Christian fellowship. *Koinonia* already and always exists by virtue of union of each Christian with Christ. Our responsibility is to devote ourselves to this existing fellowship, diligently to seek this God-created unity, to be faithful stewards of God's gift of *koinonia*.

One way in which we do this, the third practice to which the early church was devoted, is "the breaking of bread."

The breaking of bread

Luke wrote of a time before any distinction arose between the church breaking bread as part of a regular meal and the church breaking bread as a purely sacramental activity. As Willimon observes:

> In good Jewish fashion, when the blessing is said at the table, the table becomes a holy place and eating together a sacred activity. Perhaps every meal for the [early] church was experienced as an anticipation of the Messianic banquet, a foretaste of Jesus' promise that his followers would 'eat and drink at my table in my kingdom' (Luke 22:30).

Whatever our personal and corporate understandings of the Lord's Supper, whether we approach Holy Communion as a solemn memorial or a joyful feast, we benefit from the example of the earliest believers, who devoted themselves to the breaking of bread. For in the fellowship at that table we find a visible expression of the Holy Spirit at work in the new community. And as we see what the Spirit accomplished through the church that gathered in Jerusalem, we are challenged once again to realize all that the Spirit is willing to accomplish through our fellowship today.

Prayer

The fourth practice to which the earliest believers devoted themselves was prayer.

The earliest Christians may have continued to observe the traditional Jewish hours of prayer at the temple, filling this ancient practice with new meaning. Whatever the forms or content of their prayers, the members of the early church were persistent and diligent about praying. Their practice offers an example for the church in the third millennium. For, as Richard Foster writes:

> We today yearn for prayer and hide from prayer. We are attracted to it and repelled by it. We believe prayer is something we should do, even something we want to do, but it seems like a chasm stands between us and actually praying. ... My first counsel is simply a reminder that prayer is nothing more than an ongoing and growing love relationship with God the Father, Son, and Holy Spirit.

The communion of saints

As the first Christian converts gathered together and devoted themselves to the apostles' teaching, to fellowship, to the breaking of bread, and especially to prayer, a wondrous and mysterious transformation took place. By God's grace these individuals became "the holy catholic church; the communion of saints."

Thus to confess "I believe in the communion of saints" is to pledge our devotion to the apostles' teaching and to the fellowship, to the breaking of bread and to prayer.

For reflection and response

1. Name some items or individuals to which you are devoted. What about them inspires your devotion?

2. How is Christian fellowship established and maintained?

3. Why are studying the Bible, participating in the Lord's Supper, and praying essential disciplines of the Christian life?

Pray and give God thanks for the communion of the saints. You may wish to pray Psalm 133 or to use that psalm as a model for your prayer.

Scripture passages for further study
Matthew 6:9-13; Matthew 12:46-48; John 13:34-35; I Corinthians 1:1-10; I Corinthians 11:23-32.

Additional resources
Richard Foster, *Prayer: Finding the Heart's True Home* (San Francisco: HarperSanFrancisco, 1992).

Eugene Peterson, *Working the Angles: The Shape of Pastoral Integrity* (Grand Rapids, Eerdmans, 1987).

Hans Urs von Balthasar, *Prayer* (San Francisco: Ignatius Press, 1986).

Robert Webber: *Evangelicals on the Canterbury Trail*, (Waco: Jarrell, 1985).

William H. Willimon, *Acts* (Atlanta: John Knox Press, 1988).

23

THE FORGIVENESS OF SINS

Suggested Scripture reading
I John 1:1-10

Whenever Christians declare, "I believe in the forgiveness of sins," we testify – to ourselves and to the world – that our faith is in a God who is both willing and able to forgive us when we miss the mark, or when we have done that which we know we should not have done.

Such testimony is sorely needed today. Secular psychologists treat the Christian doctrine of sin as the root of much evil. Even within the church, sin, and the consequent need for forgiveness, is often downplayed to the point of invisibility. In stark contrast to such views, the Apostle John wrote:

> If we claim to be without sin, we deceive ourselves and the truth is not in us. If we confess our sins, he is faithful and just and will forgive us our sins and purify us from all unrighteousness. If we claim we have not sinned, we make him out to be a liar and his word has no place in our lives (I John 1:8-10).

In this chapter we will briefly consider five key words from this passage: confess, sin, faithful, just, and forgive.

Confess

The Greek word for "confess," *homologeo*, combines the prefix *homo*, meaning "same," with *logeo*, meaning "to say," the same root from which *logos*, "word" is derived. Thus "to confess" is "to say the same word."

While John uses this verb frequently, this is the only time he connects it with "sins." Every other confession of which John writes is a confession of faith, as, for example, in I John 4:2-3, "By this you know the Spirit of God: every spirit which confesses that Jesus Christ has come in the flesh is of God, and every spirit that does not confess Jesus is not of God" (RSV).

To confess Jesus Christ as God the Son in human flesh is to say the same word about Jesus as does God the Holy Spirit. Similarly, to confess our sins to God is to say the same word as God about our sins. Properly understood, that is a powerful concept.

In our pilgrimage of faith we sometimes make comments like, "I'm trying to know God's mind on that," or, perhaps less tactfully, "If I knew that, I'd be God." Each expression in its own way acknowledges our recognition of the biblical truth that the goal of our Christian life is to be like Christ.

This is what Paul meant when he wrote, "Your attitude should be the same as that of Christ Jesus" (Phil. 2:5) and "Do not conform any longer to the pattern of this world, but be transformed by the renewing of your mind. Then you will be able to test and approve what God's will is – his good, pleasing and perfect will" (Rom. 12:2).

To be transformed by the renewing of our minds and to have the same mind in us that was in Christ Jesus are simply other ways of acknowledging that we are called to say the same word as God says, whether we are talking about Jesus Christ or about our own sins.

"Those who deny their sin will feel no need of recourse to the cleansing power of Christ."
— *F.F. Bruce*

Sin

The New Testament uses many different words when talking about sin. Here John uses *hamartia*, which connotes "failing to hit, missing the mark." Ancient Greek philosophers originally used the term to indicate intellectual shortcomings or erroneous actions. But through its use in the Greek translation of the Old Testament, *hamartia* became widely understood in the religious sense of "sinful act," or simply, "sin." In the New Testament *hamartia* often denotes the human determination to be hostile toward God.

The consistent testimony of Scripture is that those who live in darkness, those who live outside of fellowship with God in Christ, live in opposition to God. They deceive themselves by refusing even to acknowledge that they are sinful. In short, they make God out to be a liar, allowing no place for God's Word in their lives. They refuse to say about their sins the same word God says – that their sins are real and need to be forgiven so that life-giving fellowship with God can be restored.

When we confess our sins to God, we are making a conscious and conscientious effort to say the same word God says about our sins. We are allowing God the Holy Spirit the opportunity to transform our minds, so that the mind of Christ will be our mind. We are leaving the darkness behind and walking in the light of the One who is the light of all people.

And as we confess, God forgives, for he is faithful and just.

Faithful and just

That God is faithful is one of the first things Scripture teaches us about God. The people of Israel are admonished, "Know therefore that the Lord your God is God: he is the *faithful* God, keeping his covenant to a thousand generations of those who love him and keep his commands" (Deut. 7:9). And Paul offers us one of the greatest promises in all of Scripture, "if we are faithless, [God] will remain *faithful*, for he cannot disown himself" (II Tim. 2:13).

Paul also wrote frequently about God's righteousness, God's quality of being just. The Greek word *dikaios*, which John uses here, can be translated either "righteous" or "just." The concepts of God's righteousness, God's justice, and God's justification of sinners are all expressed by this particular word.

In the Greek Old Testament, *dikaios* was often used to translate the Hebrew *hesed*, God's steadfast love, the love God shows to his people on the basis of the covenant he established with them. Isaiah, for example, speaks of God as "a righteous God and a Savior" (Isa. 45:21).

Just as God answered Israel by delivering his people from their enemies, so God will deliver us from darkness, sin, and death.

Forgive

The last word considered here, "forgive," means "to let go, to release." Originally it was a legal term used to describe the release of debtors from their debts. In the Old Testament this word was frequently used in a covenant context, as when Moses prayed "In accordance with your great love, forgive the sin of these people, just as you have *pardoned* them from the time they left Egypt until now" (Num. 14:19).

It is significant that when John writes about the forgiveness of our sins the verb "forgive" occurs only after God has been described as "faithful and just." As F.F. Bruce comments:

Those who deny their sin will feel no need of recourse to the cleansing power of Christ; those who, conscious of their sins, confess them have in Christ a Savior from whom forgiveness and cleansing from every sinful act may be freely received – not because he is indulgent and easy-going, but because he is 'faithful and just.' He is *faithful* in that his promise is sure: those who put their trust in him will not be let down; those who come to him will not be cast out. The relevance in this connection of his being *righteous* appears clearly in [I John] 2:1, where his righteousness is associated with his advocacy, 'And if anyone sin, we have an Advocate with the Father, Jesus Christ the righteous.'

The forgiveness of sins

To confess "I believe in the forgiveness of sins" is to affirm my belief that if I say the same word God says about my sins, if I admit to God that I have lost my way in the darkness and have missed the goal of a life lived in fellowship with him, then the God who is unquestionably honest, who keeps his promises forever, who always and only does what is right, will release me from the debt I have incurred, not because of what I have done, but by his mercy, through the life, death and resurrection of Jesus Christ his only Son our Lord.

May God grant us the grace to appropriate this truth each time we confess, "I believe in the forgiveness of sins."

For reflection and response

1. What does it mean to "confess" our sins?
2. Why does John connect the forgiveness of our sins with God's faithfulness and justice?
3. Why is forgiveness often difficult to accept?
4. If you have ever been released from, or finished paying off, a large debt, describe your feelings at that moment. How do those feelings match your sense of being forgiven by God?

Pray and give God thanks for the communion of the saints. You may wish to pray Psalm 51 or to use that psalm as a model for your prayer.

Scripture passages for further study

Deuteronomy 32:1-4; Isaiah 59:1-15; Matthew 6:9-15; Matthew 18:23-35; II Corinthians 5:18-21.

Additional resources

F.F. Bruce, *The Epistles of John* (Grand Rapids: Eerdmans, 1970).

Austin Farrer, *Saving Belief* (Harrisburg: Morehouse, 1994).

Bernard Ramm, *Offense to Reason: The Theology of Sin* (San Francisco: Harper & Row, 1985).

John Stott, *The Cross of Christ* (Downers Grove: InterVarsity Press, 1986).

24

THE RESURRECTION OF THE BODY

Suggested Scripture readings
I Corinthians 15:35-49; John 12:23-24

A watermelon seed does not look all that much like a watermelon. Yet when properly planted and nurtured, it develops into sweet, juicy melon that fully exhibits characteristics the seed even now embodies.

As we consider what we mean when we confess "I believe in the resurrection of the body," the picture of the seed and the plant is very helpful. For the image of a seed going into the ground and rising up as a mature plant is the first of three analogies Paul makes in I Corinthians 15 to help answer specific questions from the Corinthians about the future resurrection of believers.

Unless a kernel falls

Paul begins, "What you sow does not come to life unless it dies" (I Cor. 15:36), recalling Jesus' words, "I tell you the truth, unless a kernel of wheat falls to the ground and dies, it remains only a single seed. But if it dies, it produces many seeds" (John 12:24). Paul's concern is with death as the precondition of life, not in the sense that all must die, but in the sense that the seed itself demonstrates that out of death a new expression of life springs forth.

In response to Corinthian skepticism about the bodily resurrection, Paul insists that it is clearly possible for the dead to rise again (see Chapters 15 and 16). Jesus' resurrection proved once and for all that God's purposes are not thwarted by death. Just as a seed is buried, so is the human body. And just as a bare seed's burial leads to its resurrection – its transformation into the mature plant – so too will our present physical bodies one day be transformed from a "bare seed" into "a body as [God] has chosen" (I Cor. 15:38).

Continuity is crucial to this imagery. For the Christian as for the seed, there is only one life, but two distinctly different bodies. Even though a watermelon seed bears little physical resemblance to the mature melon, we know from experience that the plant grows from the seed. And although we lack the experience to answer the question "What kind of body will we have after the resurrection?" Scripture promises we will have "a body chosen for us by God himself."

Not all flesh is alike

In his second analogy, Paul elaborates on this theme, "All flesh is not the same: Men have one kind of flesh, animals have another, birds another and fish another. There are also heavenly bodies and there are earthly bodies; but the splendor of the heavenly bodies is one kind, and the splendor of the earthly bodies is another" (I Cor. 15:39-40).

Paul's list clearly suggests that each body is uniquely adapted to its own peculiar existence. The bodies of fish are not covered with feathers, nor are sheep covered with scales. Rather, in his creative providence, God has feathered birds that they may fly, and given fur to animals who have little shelter in sub-freezing temperatures.

Paul goes beyond these earth-bound examples by referring to "heavenly bodies." Certainly Christians living in the third millennium are far better equipped than Paul to explain the

*"So will it be with the resurrection of the dead.
The body that is sown is perishable, it is raised
imperishable; it is sown in dishonor, it is raised in
glory; it is sown in weakness, it is raised in power;
it is sown a natural body, it is raised a spiritual
body."*

— I Corinthians 15:42-43

glories of the heavens. For with our telescopes and spectrographic analysis, with our knowledge of galaxies and nebulae, asteroids and comets, pulsars and quasars, red giants, brown dwarfs and black holes, we are able to detect and describe a far greater variety of glories than Paul could have imagined.

And yet, even two millennia ago, Paul could tell that heavenly bodies differed in their glories from earthly bodies, he could tell that they differed from one another, and, most important, he could recognize that the unique glory of each was the active intention of a creative God.

Paul then applies his first two analogies, seeds and different types of glory, to the present concern of the Corinthians:

So will it be with the resurrection of the dead. The body that is sown is perishable, it is raised imperishable; it is sown in dishonor, it is raised in glory; it is sown in weakness, it is raised in power; it is sown a natural body, it is raised a spiritual body. If there is a natural body, there is also a spiritual body (I Cor. 15:42-44).

In each of these four contrasts, Paul extends the metaphor of the seed, "it is sown," then applies the language of the resurrection, "it is raised." In his fourth contrast, Paul uses the analogy of differing kinds of "bodies." Here, instead of describing how the body is sown, the adjectives "natural" and "spiritual" are used to describe respectively the body's present earthly and future heavenly expressions.

Earlier in I Corinthians, Paul used these same two words to describe the basic differences between the unbeliever and the believer. Here he describes the natural, physical body in terms of its essential characteristics as earthly, that is, belonging to the life of the present age. By contrast, the spiritual body is described as belonging to the life of the Spirit in the age to come.

Adam and Christ

Paul's final analogy compares Adam and Christ, "So it is written: 'The first man Adam became a living being;' the last Adam, a life-giving spirit. The spiritual did not come first, but the natural, and after that the spiritual" (I Cor. 15:45-46).

This quote from Genesis 2 supports Paul's claim that believers will be raised with a spiritual, that is a supernatural, body acquired through resurrection and adapted to the life of the Spirit in the coming age. Paul concludes, "As was the earthly man, so are those who are of the earth; and as is the man from heaven, so also are those who are of heaven" (I Cor. 15:48).

The verbs used in the second half of this verse are illuminating. Paul writes, "and as *is* the man from heaven" (I Cor. 15:48). Jesus Christ, the man from heaven, *is* alive. He was crucified, dead, and buried, but the third day he arose again from the dead. We can not see him or touch him, but his presence is not lessened by the limitations of our senses. To say that Jesus Christ *is* the man from heaven, is to confess our belief not only in his bodily resurrection from the dead, but in the present reality of the resurrection."

"And as *is* the man from heaven, so also *are* those who are of heaven." Present tense. Here and now. Just as you and I are of dust, just as our bodies are perishable, wearing out perhaps a bit faster than we anticipated, certainly much faster than we had hoped, so you and I, here and now, *are* those who are of heaven.

The resurrection of the body

If you are having trouble grasping the reality of your dual status as being of dust and of heaven, picture yourself trying to explain to a thin, dry, brown seed that after it has been covered with dirt, it will re-emerge a rich, round, red and white and green watermelon.

To begin with, you would face the problem of communicating with the watermelon seed. And even if you solved that one, you would have to find a way of explaining both a process and a result that the seed had never experienced, therefore could not hope to comprehend. Perhaps the only way you could effectively communicate such a remarkable transformation would be to actually become a watermelon seed, and go through the process yourself. That way, you could explain your transformation, at least to some extent, to all the watermelon seeds who would follow.

Jesus Christ, who became fully human while remaining fully God, was crucified, dead, and buried. Yet he rose again. In his resurrection Jesus acquired a spiritual body – a body freed from the constraints of the three physical dimensions, a body freed from corruption and decay, a body with all the glory of the kingdom of God.

Each time we confess "I believe in the resurrection of the body" we witness to the reality of Jesus' resurrection, and in humble confidence faithfully affirm that we will follow where he has led.

For reflection and response

1. If you have ever farmed or had a garden, describe what you have learned about God and his ways from those activities.

2. How does knowing about the resurrection of the body affect your views of life and death?

3. What does it mean to you to know that you are not merely made of dust but that even now you are of heaven?

Pray and give God thanks for the resurrection of the body. You may wish to pray Psalm 8 or to use that psalm as a model for your prayer.

Scripture passages for further study

Genesis 2:4-7; Isaiah 40:25-31; John 11:21-26; Revelation 21:1-6.

Additional resources

Diogenes Allen, *The Path of Perfect Love* (Boston: Cowley Publications, 1992).

Gordon D. Fee, *The First Epistle to the Corinthians* (Grand Rapids: Eerdmans, 1987).

Norman Geisler, *The Battle for the Resurrection* (Nashville: Thomas Nelson, 1989).

John Polkinghorne, *Serious Talk: Science and Religion in Dialogue* (London: SCM Press, 1995).

25

THE LIFE EVERLASTING

Suggested Scripture readings
Revelation 21:1-6; 22:1-7, 20

"Delete the thought of heaven from man's lexicon," writes Paul Minear, "and he is soon reduced to a one-dimensional environment, living without any invisible means of support."

Each time we recite the final affirmation of the Apostles' Creed, "I believe in ... the life everlasting," we are reminded that our lives are not limited to a single dimension. For to confess our belief in the life everlasting is to affirm that as Christians we *do* have invisible means of support, a presence and a promise that continually sustain and guide us.

The final vision of St. John's Revelation helps us reflect on God's presence here and now, and it illustrates God's promise that we will live with him forever.

Everlasting not immortal

It is important to distinguish this biblical teaching from the ancient Greek concept of immortality. Stoic philosophers taught that each individual soul had always existed and would always exist. For them, the soul's immortality required the decay of the body. As R.C. Sproul explains:

> Many people confuse the Christian concept of resurrection with the Greek view of immortality (notably, the view

articulated by Plato). The two are not synonymous. Both views affirm that there is continuity of life beyond the grave. But the differences are great. The Greek view of immortality rests its hope for eternal life on its view of the indestructible character of the soul. The soul will continue to live because it always has lived. It existed prior to birth and will continue after the body decays. The soul itself is intrinsically eternal, nonmaterial, and incapable of annihilation. To the Greek, the body is the prison house of the soul. Not until the soul is released from its captor is redemption accomplished.

The biblical doctrine of humanity contains no such pagan concept of immortality. The soul is created. It has no intrinsic self-existence apart from the creative and sustaining power of God.

'The great invisibles'

The Greek view of immortality contrasts sharply with John's final vision, which begins, "Then I saw a new heaven and a new earth" (Rev. 21:1). Eugene Peterson comments:

St. John's final vision is of heaven. It is not an ending, as we might expect, but a fresh beginning. The biblical story began, quite logically, with a beginning. Now it draws to an end, not quite so logically, also with a beginning. The sin-ruined creation of Genesis is restored in the sacrifice-renewed creation of Revelation. The product of these beginning and ending acts of creation is the same: 'the heavens and the earth' in Genesis, and 'a new heaven and a new earth' in Revelation. The story that has creation for its first word, has creation for its last word. ...

At the Genesis beginning we are immersed in materiality; at the Revelation ending we are reimmersed in materiality. ... Nothing in the gospel is presented apart from the physical. That is not to say that there is nothing but matter, for that would deny most of what living by faith asserts. But it does mean that nothing can be experienced apart from matter. The great invisibles, God and the soul, are incomprehensible apart from the great visibles, heaven and earth.

"Heaven in the gospels and the Revelation (and throughout scripture) is the metaphor that tells us that there is far more here than meets the eye."
— *Eugene Peterson*

———————————

John's vision of the new heaven and the new earth reminds us that we comprehend "the great invisibles, God and the soul" by means of what is visible, the heavens and the earth. That the first heaven and earth will be replaced by a new heaven and earth therefore indicates that God's promise of the life everlasting is not something wholly other than what we have here and now, but rather something *more*, a promise of the completion, fulfillment, perfection of God's creation.

What might this "something more" be like? John continues:

> And I heard a loud voice from the throne saying, 'Now the dwelling of God is with men, and he will live with them' (Rev. 21:3).

God with us

God's promise to be forever with his people runs throughout Scripture. God tells Abraham, "I will establish my covenant as an everlasting covenant between me and you and your descendants after you for the generations to come, to be your God and the God of your descendants after you" (Gen. 17:7). He repeats this promise to Moses, "I will take you as my own people, and I will be your God. Then you will know that I am the Lord your God, who brought you out from under the yoke of the Egyptians" (Ex. 6:7). And God declares of his people, "I will give them a heart to know me, that I am the Lord. They will be my people, and I will be their God, for they will return to me with all their heart" (Jer. 24:7).

Our creaturely inability to experience the fullness of God's presence in this age, and God's promise of that fullness in the age to come, finds perhaps its best-known expression in I Corinthians 13:12, "Now we see but a poor reflection as in a mirror; then we shall see face to face. Now I know in part; then I shall know fully, even as I am fully known."

In the new heaven and the new earth, when we enter into the fullness of the life everlasting, we will have the "more" that John envisioned, for then we shall see God face to face; then we shall fully know, even as we are fully known. We do not need to doubt this longed-for future reality, for the one who said to John "I am making everything new!" also said, "I am the Alpha and the Omega, the Beginning and the End" (Rev. 21:6).

Heaven

The longing for the Lord's return, for the fullness of age to come, has always been at the heart of Christian faith and life, for his return will inaugurate our full participation in the life everlasting. Another description of the life everlasting is "heaven." Eugene Peterson writes:

> Heaven in the gospels and the Revelation (and throughout scripture) is the metaphor that tells us that there is far more here than meets the eye. Beyond and through what we see there is that which we cannot see, and which is, wondrously, not 'out there' but right here before us and among us; *God* – his rule, his love, his judgment, his salvation, his mercy, his grace, his healing, his wisdom.

> Calling the word *heaven* a metaphor does not make it less real; it simply recognizes that it is a reality inaccessible at this point to any of our five senses. The Hebrews and Greeks made one word do the work for which English employs two. *Shamayim* (Hebrew) and *ouranos* (Greek) mean either the visible sky over us or the invisible realm of God invading us, with the context determining which sense is being expressed. ... The biblical 'heaven' doing double duty for the visible

and the invisible, keeps our imaginations at work making connections between what we see and do not see, both of them equally real, each a reminder of the other.

The life everlasting

Heaven, the life everlasting, is a present reality, one that lies just beyond our comprehension. Therefore we need reminders, images, analogies, connections between the life we live and the life everlasting. If we work at being alert, we can find the hints of this life all around us every day. Supremely we find such reminders in our worship, which often includes the public recitation of the Apostles' Creed.

Our affirmation "I believe in the life everlasting," like the word "heaven" for which it is a synonym, does "double duty for the visible and the invisible, keep[ing] our imaginations at work making connections between what we see and do not see, both of them equally real, each a reminder of the other."

Thus we are reminded that we will spend eternity in the presence of Almighty God each time we confess "I believe in the life everlasting."

For reflection and response

1. Why may the final visions of Revelation be described as "a beginning?"
2. What do you think heaven will be like? How did you arrive at that answer?
3. How do the glimpses of heaven offered by John help us in our life on earth?

Pray and give God thanks for the communion of the saints. You may wish to pray Psalm 103 or to use that psalm as a model for your prayer.

Scripture passages for further study

Genesis 1:1-2:9; Genesis 3:22-24; Jeremiah 31:31-34; Hebrews 11:1-3; Revelation 1:1-8.

Additional resources

Thomas C. Oden, *Life in the Spirit: Systematic Theology: vol. 3* (San Francisco: HarperSanFrancisco, 1994).

Eugene Peterson, *Reversed Thunder: Revelation and the Praying Imagination of St. John* (San Francisco: Harper & Row, 1988).

R.C. Sproul, *Renewing Your Mind* (Grand Rapids: Baker, 1998).

26
AMEN

Suggested Scripture readings
Isaiah 65:15-16; John 3:1-16; Revelation 3:14, 22:18-21

In Chapter 1 we asked, "What does it mean for a Christian to say 'I believe?'" a phrase that translates the single Latin word *credo*. In this concluding chapter we will begin by looking at the single Hebrew word *amen*. *Amen* is an especially appropriate conclusion to a creed, for it recalls those beliefs we have confessed, and in so doing draws us toward a life of faithful action.

Amen in the Old Testament

Amen is said and heard so many times in Christian worship that we may overlook the word's origin and significance. *Amen* comes from the Hebrew root *aman*, which connotes firmness, reliability, or certainty. In its various grammatical forms the word can mean "to cause to be certain," "to be assured," "to be established," and "one who is faithful, sure, dependable."

While the verb *aman* is found 100 times in the Old Testament, its derivative form *amen* (as both Greek and English transliterate the Hebrew) occurs only 27 times, usually as the response of an individual or the whole assembly to words spoken by another. The prophets or the people of Israel said "amen" to acknowledge the validity and the binding nature of the words spoken by others – a prayer (I Chron. 16:36), a curse (Deut. 27:14-26), or a doxology (Ps. 41:13). In such circumstances it might be paraphrased, "Yes, we agree," or "May it be as you have said."

A unique Old Testament use of *amen* comes in Isaiah 65:16. There, in the context of prophecies of judgment and salvation, after declaring that God will give his servants a new name, Isaiah writes, "Whoever invokes a blessing in the land will do so by the God of truth [the *amen*]; he who takes an oath in the land will swear by the God of truth [the *amen*]." Because God is supremely reliable and trustworthy, God himself is named *Amen*.

Amen in the New Testament

Apart from the gospels, the New Testament use of *amen* follows the Old Testament pattern. Often when Paul bursts into praise of God the Father or God the Son, he closes his doxology with *amen*. *Amen* also concludes several hymns of praise in Revelation. At the end of Revelation, the Apostle John adds his own *amen*, attesting to the validity of what he has seen and heard and offering his hope for its fulfillment.

And in Revelation 3:14, speaking to the church in Laodicea, the risen Christ declares, "These are the words of the *Amen*, the faithful and true witness, the ruler of God's creation." In this self-revelation to the Laodiceans, Jesus takes for himself the very name used of God in Isaiah 65, an unmistakable assertion of his deity.

Jesus' use of *amen*

In the gospels, *amen* is also found 100 times, always spoken by Jesus. Jesus, however, never applied it to another person's statement. Instead, he often prefaced his own teachings with the expression, "*Amen* I say to you," a phrase apparently intended to emphasize the truth and the importance of the

*"The Creed's final 'Amen' repeats and confirms its
first words: 'I believe.' To believe is to say 'Amen'
to God's words, promises and commandments."*
— Catechism of the Catholic Church

---

words he was preparing to speak. No one else in the New Testament is recorded using this verbal formulation, and no exact Hebrew equivalent of this saying has been found in any prior or contemporaneous literature.

In John 3:3 and 3:5 Jesus begins with "*Amen, amen* I say to you." Various English translations render this double *amen* as "Verily, verily," "Truly, truly," "Very truly," and, as in the New International Version, "I tell you the truth." Here, as throughout the gospels, Jesus is using this phrase in the context of correcting errors. He offers no proof of his words other than his own authority, implying that his words, like those of his Father, are true by virtue of the fact that he says them. Later in John 3, John the Baptist testifies of Jesus, "For the one whom God has sent speaks the words of God, for God gives the Spirit without limit" (John 3:34). Thus, as Gerald Hawthorne notes, Jesus' use of *amen* was intended:

> not so much to direct attention to his divinity as to his authority to speak for God as *the* messenger of God. ... the closest analogy to his 'Amen, I say to you' is the formula so frequently used by those who spoke the words of God in the Old Testament – 'Thus says the Lord' – that expression of the prophets by which they made clear that their words were God's. ...

> With the words 'Amen, I say to you,' Jesus certainly went beyond the Old Testament prophets because he, unlike them, had been given the Spirit without measure (John 3:34). Like them, however, he was in essence saying the same thing but

in a higher key: 'You must listen to what I have to say, because the words that I speak are not mine; they are the very words of God' (John 3:34).

Making God's words our words

Making sure that our words are also God's words is still a worthy goal. And the Apostles' Creed is a worthy tool for helping us reach that goal. In Chapter 2 we noted that creeds served three purposes: Definition – giving Christians a way of understanding and proclaiming, "This is what I believe;" Defense – giving Christians a standard for distinguishing distortion, or heresy, from truth; and Declaration – a means by which we can declare, to ourselves and to the world, what it is that we believe.

Chapter 1 focused on the nature of faith and observed:

To say 'I believe' is to give intellectual assent to the fundamental doctrines of the Christian faith: that God is our Father, the creator of the heavens and the earth; that Jesus is his only Son, our only Savior; that the ongoing ministry of the Holy Spirit makes us one with God and with each other.

To say "I believe" is also to give evidence of our attitude of trust, an attitude that says to God: I will step out in faith, trusting you to guide my steps; I will return good for evil, trusting your goodness and your mercy; I will follow your call through the lonely places, trusting the promise of your presence with me, now and in the life to come.

And finally, to say 'I believe' is to act. It is to put our intellectual assent and our attitude of trust into faithful action in our daily lives.

I Believe … Amen

The *Catechism of the Catholic Church* conveys the Creed's capacity to encourage faithful action when it observes:

The Creed's final 'Amen' repeats and confirms its first words: 'I believe.' To believe is to say 'Amen' to God's words, promises and commandments; to entrust oneself completely to him who is the 'Amen' of infinite love and perfect faithfulness. The Christian's everyday life will then be the 'Amen' to the 'I believe' of our baptismal profession of faith.

Bounded by "I believe" and "amen," The Apostles' Creed reminds us that Christian faith is not ours to create. Rather, our work is to add our own *amen* to "the faith that was once for all entrusted to the saints" (Jude 3).

Amen.

For reflection and response

1. What is the difference between Jesus' use of "amen" and others' uses of that word?
2. Why is "amen" an appropriate word with which to end the Apostles' Creed?
3. Do you say "amen" at the end of your prayers? If so, why?
4. In daily Christian faith and life, what is the connection between "I believe" and "amen?"

Pray and give God thanks for all he has revealed about himself and his love for us. You may wish to pray Psalm 19 or to use that psalm as a model for your prayer.

Scripture passages for further study

Matthew 13:17; Matthew 16:24-28; John 15:19-26; II Corinthians 1:16-20.

Additional resources

John Brokhoff, *This You Can Believe: A New Look at the Apostles' Creed* (Lima, Ohio: C.S.S. Publishing, 1987).

Catechism of the Catholic Church (Mahwah, NJ, Paulist Press, 1994).

Walter A. Elwell, ed., *Evangelical Dictionary of Biblical Theology* (Grand Rapids: Baker, 1996).

Jack B. Scott, "*'aman*," in *Theological Wordbook of the Old Testament* (Chicago: Moody Press, 1980).

Gerald F. Hawthorne, "Amen," in *Dictionary of Jesus and the Gospels* (Downers Grove: InterVarsity Press, 1992).

Resources for Renewal

FROM PLC PUBLICATIONS

Standing Firm: Reclaiming Christian Faith in Times of Controversy **By Parker T. Williamson**

Standing Firm is a riveting account of how the Nicene Creed emerged out of fourth-century controversies over the deity of Christ. With clarity and passion, Williamson traces our modern religious concerns to the past and finds hope and resolution for the future.

Thomas F. Torrance, professor emeritus of theology at Edinburgh, Scotland, calls *Standing Firm* "one of the most brilliant, refreshing and helpful books concerned with the heart and centre of the life and witness of the church that has happened in recent years."

An excellent resource for church study groups. Single copies: $12. Ten or more copies: $6 each. Plus shipping and handling.

Whom Alone We Worship and Serve: What the Bible Teaches about God **By Robert P. Mills**

This exciting new Bible study blends first-rate scholarship, devotional insight and practical application. The text feeds the soul, fires the heart and sharpens the mind. *Whom Alone* interweaves the witness of Scripture, the insights of scholars from early church fathers to current evangelical commentators, and the historic Reformed perspective. It is designed for use by Sunday school classes, Presbyterian Women and other groups.

Single copies: $4.50. Ten or more copies: $4 each. Plus shipping and handling.

To order copies call toll-free: **1-800-368-0110**
PLC Publications • PO Box 2210 • Lenoir, NC 28645-2210